Historic Walking Guides

Bruges

DestinWorld
publishing

First Edition 2009

Edited by Zöe Wildsmith
Cover design by John Wright

ISBN 978-0-9559281-1-6

British Library Cataloguing-in-Publication Data
A catalogue record for this book is available from the British Library.

Published by Destinworld Publishing Ltd.
www.destinworld.com

Table of contents

Foreword

I have travelled all over the world but when people ask me my favourite city, I don't hesitate when I say Bruges. I first visited Bruges in 1990 while touring Belgium with my sister and immediately felt like I'd come home. I fell in love with the cobbled streets, the canals and the entire atmosphere that surrounds it. There is so much history, but yet, it is still so very alive.

In the early days, I would just stick a map in my back pocket and try to get lost. Now I feel like every nook and cranny is an old friend, though inevitably, I discover something new on each trip. I've been back countless times to wander—taking friends and family and sometimes just escaping on my own.

Big enough to lose yourself, but small enough to be familiar, it's a city steeped in history and beauty to be enjoyed at any time of year.

While there are numerous walking guides to Bruges, I have tried to replicate the walks that I feel are the most logical and also allow you to see the most. The first walk is designed for day trippers. It covers a lot of territory, but you will see the quintessential Bruges. The second walk is for people who have a second day, or want to just get away from the more touristy areas. Walk three takes you to more quiet regions of Bruges by exploring the ring of the "egg". Of course the Chocolate Walk and the Historic Beer Walk are for pure enjoyment.

The end section offers practical information you may need while here—such as telephone numbers, ongoing events, etc. It also includes a quick reference for churches and museums covered in the walks, in addition to ones you may want to explore on your own.

Wander the streets and you'll see what I mean about Bruges' charm and appeal. It's an open book for historians, a photographer's dream and a place to roam time and time again.

Janice McDonald

Introduction to Bruges

P art pedestrian, part canals, all magical—this is Bruges, Belgium. A small city near the coast, Bruges is often overlooked by those searching for bigger cities to explore. But once you visit, you'll want to come back time and time again.

Located in Belgium's Flemish region, Bruges is the capital and the largest city in the province of West Flanders. You will see the name written as Bruges—the French spelling—and Brugge—which is the Flemish. Both are derived from a combination of the Old Norse term Bryggja, which means "landing stage"—homage to its history as a seaport—and the old English word byrcg, which means "bridge".

Since this is a city of canals, there are plenty of bridges to be crossed. The current count in the heart of the city is 43, but in Bruges' heyday as a port in the 16th century, there were as many as 68.

UNESCO gave Bruges' historic centre World Heritage status in 2000 and one could argue that no city deserves it more. Dating back to the 9th century, as you explore this quaint Belgian city, you will find yourself staring at homes built almost as long ago. Many boast their age in wrought iron on their façades. Most of Bruges' medieval architecture remains intact. In some of the neighbourhoods, it's as if time stood still a few hundred years ago, with only telltale modern conveniences giving away the current age.

While the city itself expands across a fair sized region, what visitors come to see is the historical centre, which is ringed by both a canal and a road. It's just 7km (4mi) to walk around the entire distance so crisscrossing to pick out your highlights is quite easy to do. And there are so many to choose from! No other town in Northern Europe can boast so many historical monuments. The canals themselves offer some of the most enchanting scenery you will ever find. Around every corner is another snapshot to be captured.

Its nickname is "Venice of the North", but Bruges is truly a city apart from any other. Whether your interests are churches, museums or just soaking up the ambience, there is plenty to keep you occupied. Add to those interests world class cuisine, a beer culture that draws people from across the globe to sip... and of course the chocolate for which Belgium is so famous.

The churches scattered around Bruges cover every denomination with some dating back more than a millennium. Visitors would be astounded by the unique offerings of each—from the J. Van Oost painting in the church located in the Beguinage convent to the Michelangelo pieta of the Cathedral of Our Lady, to the purported remnant of Christ's garment at the Church of the Holy Blood.

Museums range from the historical, like the former palace of the Lords of Gruuthuse, to the quirky, like the French Fry Museum. Prepare to be astounded by just how many of the things with which you are familiar that actually have their roots in Bruges.

But most of all, Bruges exudes an atmosphere that is to be simply absorbed and enjoyed. So take your time as you wander around and breathe in its history and culture—you know you will be back!

Getting There, Getting Around

As the capital of West Flanders, there is easy access to Bruges via car, rail and bus from just about anywhere in Belgium and beyond. The inner historical ring is often called "the egg" because of its shape. The egg has ten points of entry and most of these points coincide with the former historical city gates that helped protect Bruges for almost 600 years.

Driving

The thing to remember most is that Bruges is largely a pedestrian friendly town and the local municipality wants to keep it that way. Parking is at premium and most streets are one way. Traffic management has done this on purpose to discourage driving. The main routes into the city lead directly to car parks and its best to take advantage of them and take your tour of Bruges on foot. Free public transport is available for those who park their cars in the main railway station car park.

If you are arriving from Brussels, you will likely come in at the south-west corner of Bruges via E40-A10. You will enter the city right next to the railway station through an area called Boeveriepoort. Take a right turn onto Buiten Begijnevest and park in the Bruges Railway station car park for free. Or, you can cross the roundabout and take Koning Albert I Lian to a public parking area at 't Zand, a plaza flanked by hotels and restaurants.

If you feel lucky about parking and want to venture further into the heart of the city, turn right on Zuidzandstraat. Just past Sint Salvatorskathedraal, the road changes name to Steenstraadt. Soon afterwards, you will find yourself right in the middle of Markt.

Coming from Zeebrugge and Calais, you will also be on E10-A10. You will enter the city on the north-west side through an area called Bloedput and will be on Hoefijzerlaan after you cross the canal. When you pass Smeden-straat, you will see the public parking on your left. Turn in here to park, or turn left to go around 't Zand to be able to turn on Zuidzandstraat. If you stay straight, the railway station will be on your right in just a few hundred yards once you pass the roundabout. Parking here is your best bet.

From Rotterdam, Antwerp or Knokke, you will enter the city on the north-east corner via N374. This route means you enter through Dampoort and will take you onto Langerei, directly along the canal, which was Bruges' original harbour.

Bus

Belgium has an extensive network of bus routes and most are quite inexpensive if you can afford the time to figure them out. Transit buses arrive in Bruges at the railway station. There is a kiosk at the station where you can purchase tickets or you can buy them on the bus itself.

There are two types of tickets available:

- De lijnkaart (line card): for trips outside the city.
- De stadskaart (city card): for trips inside the city.

Bus links to the Markt are frequent, although the Markt is only about a 20-minute walk from the station.

Cycling

There are far more bikes in Bruges than cars and for good reason. They are much easier to manoeuvre and you can actually get around the city faster via bike. There are several places in Bruges where you can rent a bike during your stay. The bouncing on the cobblestones may take its toll, but it's an adventure worth experiencing.

Cars are required to give way to pedestrians and cyclists and two-way cycling is allowed on many of the one-way streets.

Canal Tour

Although walking is the best way to see Bruges, taking a canal tour of the city is almost a necessity. The tours run from March-November from 10am-6pm. Trips last 30 minutes and leave from one of five designated points in the city:

- Georges Stael – Katelijnestraat 4
- Gruuthuse at the corner of Drijver and Nieuwstraat
- De Meulemeester near the bridge at Wollestraat,
- Michielssens – Huidenvettersplein behind the Burg
- Coudenys – Rozenhoedkaai

Horse-Drawn Cab

Horse-drawn cabs leave from the Markt Square and from Wijn

Horse-drawn cabs leave from the Markt Square and from Wijngaardstraat near the Beguinage. Tours last half an hour, including a short stop at the Beguinage.

Plane

There is no aeroplane service directly to Bruges but the city can easily be reached by flying to Brussels (also called Brussels National), Brussels South Charleroi or Lille. There are frequent coach and bus connections between the two Brussels airports and Bruges.

Rail

Train is one of the most popular ways for tourists to visit Bruges. The city's main railway station is located just on the outside of the city egg and is within walking distance of most of the key historic sites as well as being near a host of hotels. The station is serviced by Belgian Railways (NMBS), which means it is connected to all major Belgian cities.

Trains to and from Brussels run about every half hour, so there is no need for reservation. The trip takes about an hour. Conveniently, there are also trains directly from Brussels Airport to Brussels City Centre where you can change trains at Brussels Midi and go directly to Bruges.

Taxis

Taxis are plentiful but in general need to be booked in advance. There is a €4,50 minimum charge so if you can walk to a location, do. There are taxi stands at the railway station and also in the Markt. The numbers are:

- Markt – 32 50 33 44 44
- Stationsplein – 32 50 38 46 50

History

W alk along the charming maze of canals that criss-cross Bruges and it's easy to understand how water has played an important role in the city's history. At one time, this was the largest seaport in Europe.

The earliest settlements here were Gaelic-Roman about 2,000 years ago. While fortifications helped cement the Romans' claim to the region, inhabitants were busy establishing a small trade centre. It's believed the area remained inhabited throughout this entire period until the Germanic people attacked the Flemish coastal plain around 270. By the time Saint Eligius began his efforts to spread Christianity to this part of Europe, Bruges was believed to be the most important fortification in the region.

Bruges first began getting world attention in the 7th century when the Counts of Flanders made the settlement their residence. This is also when the city got its name. Early trade with Scandinavians earned the town the Old Norse name Bryggja, which means "landing stage". Combined with the old English word byrcg, which means "bridge", it began appearing on maps as Bruges.

Known for their business acumen, the Counts of Flanders took advantage of the harbour on the River Zwin next to their fortress-like Burg and before long the tiny city was expanding. It soon became a thriving port as well as the chief trading and financial centre of northern Europe.

But nature paid a cruel trick on the city's success. Around 1050, silt in the River Reie cut Bruges off from its main access to the sea. There was a reprieve from financial disaster in 1134 when a fluke tidal wave changed the entire terrain of the Flemish Coastal plain, opening a direct access to the sea through the Zwin. In the meantime, the city worked to divert waters of the Reie into a network of reitjes, or canals, within the city.

By then, Bruges was officially known as a city, having been granted a charter in 1128. The residents celebrated by building a wall around the city to protect it from outsiders, establishing nine gates for points of entry.

By 1300, there were more people living in Bruges than in Paris. In fact, with a population of about 45,000, there were twice as many residents living in the historical city centre than currently reside in the same area.

Throughout the Middle Ages, Bruges remained on top in its status as the richest city in Northern Europe. Best known for being capital of the Flemish woollen industry, the city thrived with the manufacturing of not only the high quality wool, but a host of other products. The streets were bustling with merchants, their customers and craftsmen.

A merger of the dynasties of Flanders and Burgundy saw Bruges push towards the production of more luxury goods, while arts and culture flourished. The sudden death of the Duke of Burgundy in 1482 prompted a revolt against his widow and from there, the city's fortunes saw a downward spiral from which it never fully recovered. While trade continued, it was on a far smaller scale and the silting of its ships' channel only exacerbated the problem.

The city began trying to fill in some of the canals or at least build over them but simply ran out of funds. By the mid 19th century, Bruges was considered the poorest city in the region.

That lack of prosperity is perhaps what helped it become what it is today. From the early 17th century, time virtually stopped within the old city. Its medieval architecture remained intact, untouched by modern expansion. In the late 19th century, tourists and artists began rediscovering Bruges' charms.

A new seaport that opened in 1907 in Zeebrugge helped re-introduce visitors to the almost forgotten city. Word began to spread of the existence of this unspoiled historical gem and its scenic buildings, bridges, canals and monuments.

As late as the 1970s, the residents were just beginning to catch on to their potential and undertook a massive cleanup of the canals which were still being used as open sewers. Drainage into them was finally halted and silt and debris were removed. In general, the canals are now about 2m deep. Fish once again thrive in them, as do the swans for which Bruges is known.

In 2000, The United Nations Educational, Scientific and Cultural Organization (UNESCO) granted Bruges' historic city centre the classification of World Heritage Site, honouring the beauty and history that millions of visitors come to experience each year.

The Walks

Only about an hour from Brussels either by train or car, Bruges is the perfect alternative to the "Big City" and the perfect city to take a stroll through history. Because the historical centre is ringed by canals and a road, it's easy to wander and never really get lost.

These walks are designed to guide you through the specific sections or specific interests within the city. You can enjoy as much or as little of each as you'd like. It's easy to hop off and just sit and enjoy your surroundings at any time. The ring around the city is just 7km (4mi), so there is much that can be seen in a relatively small area.

Walk I leaves from the train station and gives a good introduction to Bruges. This covers the most noted sites and places and shows you their history. It is an easy walk for day trippers.

Walk II leaves from the Markt in the centre of town and heads into the northern neighbourhoods. This walk is quieter and less touristy but just as rich in history.

Walk III takes you on the outer ring along what used to be the walls of the city. Here is where you will find what is left of the city gates and the windmills. You'll see canals and also visit some neighbourhoods that are off the beaten path.

Walk IV is for chocolate lovers. You have to really pace yourself to do this, but you get to enjoy some great chocolate while still seeing the city.

Walk V could easily end up as a crawl. Bruges is a beer lover's dream and this walk is laid out to allow you to visit and experience some of the city's best offerings in the way of pubs, restaurants and beer shops.

If arriving by train, all you need to do is exit the station, cross the Buiten Begijnenvest ring road and you are there. If you are driving to Bruges, you will arrive via one of ten access points from the ring road that surrounds the city. The obvious place to head after you arrive is the City Centre, where the Belfry and Markt Square or Grande Place are located.

Welcome to Bruges. Or, as they say in Flemish, Welkom.

– Walk I –
From the Train Station

Since many visitors just hop on a train from Brussels and the easiest parking option is at the train station, this walk is designed for those who want to see the quintessential Bruges.

When you exit the train station, or its car park, you should cross over the four lane road called Buiten Begijnenvest. There will be large green areas with footpaths on the other side. Head left and in a short walk, you will see the street Oostmeirs. Turn right and immediately take the pedestrian area to the right at the brick wall along the tree lined Begijnenvest. There will be a canal on your right.

The path intersects a body of water called the Lake of Love and there will be a tower on your right. A pedestrian bridge is directly in front of you and it crosses what used to be the mouth of Bruges inner harbour.

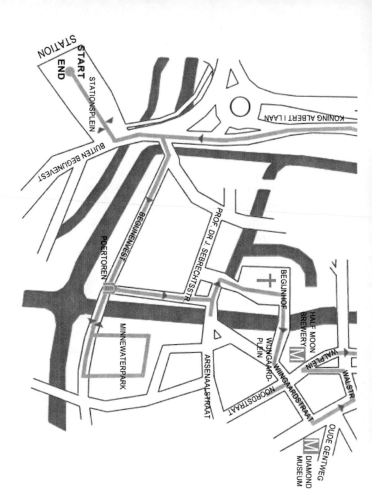

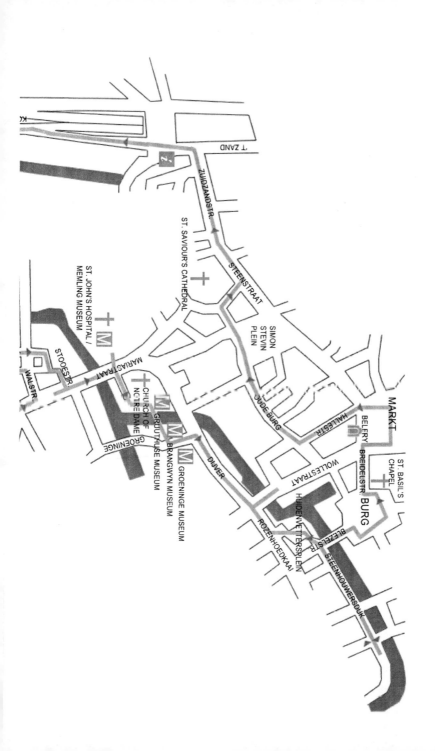

The Lake of Love

Once the inner harbour of Bruges, the Lake of Love is where the Reie River entered the city. The lake may look small, but in medieval times Bruges received up to 150 ships a day in this and the harbour on the opposite side of town. Barges transporting people from Ghent used to come into the city here after their eight-hour journey. The lake itself was created around 1200 when locks were built.

Legend has it that the Lake of Love got its name through the troubles of a woman named Minna who was promised to one man while loving another. She fled her father and died here on the banks where her lover later found her. The story says that he moved the river so that he could bury her beneath the waters. Another fable has it that the lake is home to a "min" or water sprites who play love songs to spark romance among couples who venture near.

Poertoren

The three-storey brick tower next to the bridge at the corner of the Begijnenvest is part of the original defensive wall that surrounded Bruges for centuries. This tower is called the Poertoren and was built in 1398. A defensive tower from the original city walls, it was used for gunpowder storage. An identical tower used to be directly opposite on the other side of the bridge.

Minnewaterpark

If you choose to cross the bridge, you will be in Minnewaterpark. Built in 1979 on what used to be the site of old castle grounds, Minnewaterpark is the site of the annual Cactus Festival each July, which features national and international artists and musicians. The castle is long since gone but the porter's lodge and gardens remain.

Cross back over the bridge and walk the path along the Lake of Love until you get to the Lock House.

Minnewaterliniek

On your left are the walls of Minnewaterliniek, a residential care home. The walls are the longest outer rampart in all of Bruges today.

The Lock House (Saishuise or Sluice Gate)

The Lock House was built in the 1500s to help control the flow of water into Bruges' inner canals and to keep them at a constant depth for the barges that came here. In the 1970s the locks were closed to keep the pollution that was in the main canals from entering the city. The scene in front of the Lock House is probably one of the most recognizable views of Bruges there is. The canals in front of you are always filled with swans and the Beguinage convent and bridge create a memorable tableau.

The Swans of Bruges

The swans in this small lake have become symbols of Bruges. Their ancestors have been chasing each other and tourists around these waters since 1488. Legend has it that the townsfolk executed an administrator named Pieter Lanchals. (Lanchals means "long neck" and the family coat of arms was a swan.) Lanchals belonged to the court of Maximilian of Austria, husband and successor of duchess Mary of Burgundy. Maximilian didn't take kindly to the killing of his courtier and he ordered the city to keep swans on its waters for eternity. The swans are officially property of the city and are marked on their beaks with a capital "B" and the date of their birth.

Facing the swan-filled lake, with the Lock House at your back, turn left and take Arsenaalstraat until it becomes a dead end at the sign for the Beguinage or Monastery de Wijngaard.

Beguinage (Monastery de Wijngaard)

Silence is revered here in what is still a working convent and from time to time you can still see nuns in their black and white habits walking across the whitewashed building-lined courtyard. It's called several things including Begijnhof, Beguinage and Monastery de Wijngaard, but the "Princely Beguinage of the Vineyard" was originally founded in 1245 by Margaret of Constantinople, Countess of Flanders. The Beguins allowed women to lead a religious life without having to join the order and retreat from the rest of the world. They made their living in the lace and wool industries.

Since 1930, the community has been maintained by Benedictine Nuns. Inside the courtyard, in addition to the houses is the Beguinage Church, built in the 14th century. It's dedicated to Saint Elizabeth and is adorned with original works by J. Van OoSt (Learn more about this and other churches in the Churches section at the back of the book.)

Just past the church, near the gate is a small house museum. The Beguine's House, with its simple kitchen, living room, bedroom and inner garden, provides a good picture of the day-to-day life of the former inhabitants.

When you exit the Beguine's House, turn right and pass through the main gate onto the bridge

The Gate and Bridge

The original bridge was constructed in 1298. It was replaced in 1570 by the present day triple arched footbridge of stone. The gate to the Beguinage was built in 1776 and is adorned with the date in wrought iron as well as a statue commemorating Saint Elizabeth to whom the convent is dedicated. There are only two entrances to the Beguinage; the one you entered through

earlier and this one. This park area in front of the bridge is one of the most popular for people to go and sit and watch the swans. You can also catch a carriage ride here for a brief tour around town.

When you come off the bridge, go past the fountain with the horse's heads spewing water. The pump was created in 1982 by Jef Claerhout. Turn left on Wijngaardstraat and at the next street on your right, take a small detour down Noordstraadt.

Almshouse (Godshuis) De Vos (1713) − Noordstraat

On your right you will see an old housing complex with a low-walled flowered courtyard in front of it. On the house in iron numbers is "1713". This is the Almshouse de Vos.

At one time, there were more than 260 Almshouses in Bruges. Built by both guilds and the rich to administer funds to the poor, most were simply one-room buildings. De Vos had eight houses originally, and a chapel. There is no entrance allowed because it is now owned by the city and houses the elderly.

Walk back towards Wijngaardstraat and turn right. Go about 100m and cross left over Katelijnestraat to the corner of Oud Gentweg.

Diamond Museum (Diamantmuseum) − Katelijnestraat 43

The Belgian colony of the Congo was a huge source of the world's diamonds in the 14th and 15th centuries and they were brought to Bruges to be cut. It was the first northern European diamond centre, well before Antwerp or Amsterdam. The Diamantmuseum is one of only five diamond museums in the world and it is the only one where diamonds continue to be cut and polished daily. (Learn more about this and other museums in the Museums section at the back of the book.)

Cross back over Katelijnestraat and turn left on Walstraat. Within a couple of metres you'll see two squares; one on either side of the street. This area is called Walplein. Turn left and stay on the right side of the square and you will find Bruges' only remaining brewery.

Half Moon Brewery (Brewery De Halve Maan) − Walplein 26

A brewery has stood on this site since the 16th century. Half Moon Brewery was founded in 1856 by Henry Maes and is still run by his descendents. You enter the gates and are immediately in a courtyard. In the summer you can have drinks here, or there is always the option of the restaurant. Better yet, take the hour tour. It's an interesting presentation and the trip to the roof provides a fabulous panorama of the city. While the beer is brewed here, it is aged and bottled elsewhere because there isn't enough space to meet the growing demands.

The Brewery itself has been modernized and what used to take 50 people to accomplish can now be handled by the brew master and three assistants. Take your time to taste a Brugse Zot beer. Zot means "lunatic" and after a few, you'll understand why it gets the name! Belgium is known for its beer and as early as 100 years ago there were 28 breweries in Bruges. Half Moon Half Moon is the lone remainder. (The Brewery is featured in Walk V – Historic Beer.)

When you exit Half Moon, turn left and cross back over Walstraat to the other small square. You will see a small alley on the left hand side. Go through the alley.

Stoofstraat

The small alley on the north side of Walplein is called Stoofstraat and it's the narrowest street in Bruges. It also has one of the most risqué reputations in town. Stoofstraat means "Stove Street" because stoves were used to heat the Turkish baths that were here in the early 1400s. Now lined with quaint craft shops, back then the baths were a front for prostitution. Notice the tile rendering of the illicit activities on your right as your exit the alley.

When you get to Katelijnestraat, turn right just to see this building

Rooms Convent Almshouse – 9-19 Katelijnestraat

A white building that stands out because of its white façade against the other red brick buildings is the Rooms Convent. The building is very plain except the name and the year 1330 painted on the front. This is the city's oldest almshouse still in existence.

Head back from where you came, cross over the canal. From the bridge you will notice a boat dock where you can take a tour of the canals of Bruges.

Boat Landing G. Stael Katelijnestraat 4

This is one of just five landings throughout the city where you can take your canal tour. Opposite the dock is St John's Church, associated with St John's Hospital.

Continue over the bridge on Katelijnestraat and turn right through the passageway into the former St John's Hospital area.

St John's Hospital − Oud Sint Jan

Used as a hospital from 1188 until 1978, the huge complex houses a nunnery, a friars' abbey, medieval infirmaries, an old pharmacy and the Memling Museum, which is famous for its works by Flemish artist Hans Memling.
The highlight of the museum is something called the Ursula Shrine, which is a wooden reliquary depicting the life of 4th Century Breton princess and martyr Ursula. According to legend, the decorated coffer contains not only Ursula's ashes, but those of 11,000 virgins who died with her. The Memling is part of the Bruggemusea, which is a city-run chain of museums throughout Bruges. Each of the museums has a theme according to its location.
The Hospital compound is a popular tour stop and there are tours that deal entirely with St John's. The restored buildings are now home to the Art and Congress Centre as well as some of the Bruges Tourism Offices. They are also used today by the Oud Sint-Jan Foundation for exhibitions and conventions.

Cross over Katelijnestraat.

The Church of Our Lady (Notre Dame) − Onze-Lieve-Vrouwekerk

With a 122-m brick spire towering above, the Church of Our Lady dominates the Bruges Skyline. The tallest building in Bruges, it is also the second tallest brick structure in the world. Although the spire is noteworthy for little more than its size, the Church of Notre Dame has been a part of Bruges' history for more than 1,000 years. The first chapel was built here on the foundation of a 7th century church.

The bed of the canal behind the grounds was actually moved to accommodate the church's expansion, a matter that also moved the house of prayer into Brugean territory whereas before it was in Sijsele.

While there are quaint gardens with ancient grapevines on the exterior, Our Lady is known for what lies inside. In 1514, merchant brothers Jan and Alexander Mouscron returned from Italy with a white marble sculpture of the Madonna and Child created by Michelangelo in 1504 and donated it to the church. It's believed the pieta was originally intended for the cathedral in Sienna, Italy.

The interior of the church is worth exploring for its rich, wooden carvings and noteworthy paintings in each of its chapels. In the choir space behind the high altar you can also find the tombs of Charles the Bold who was the last Valois Duke of Burgundy, and his daughter, the Duchess Mary. Mary united two dynasties when she married Maximilian of Austria. The church is free but there is a small fee for the museum, which is also a Bruggemusea.

Exit the church through the door you entered and go round to the back of the church. Cross over the bridge.

Saint Boniface Bridge (Sint-Bonifaciutsbrug)

This picturesque stone bridge may look old, but it was really built in 1910. If you look down, you will notice two stone platforms beneath the bridge. This is all that remains of what was once a lock that was used to control water levels in the canal. On the brick wall on the opposite side of the canal you will notice a stone sailing ship. It was taken from an inn in Nieuwpoort when the bridge was built.

Coming through the archway after the bridge, you will enter a walled park area. To the right is the Brangwyn-Arenthuis and to the left is the Gruuthuse Museum.

Historical Museum Gruuthuse – Dijver 17

This city palace is definitely worth a look. Another of the Bruggemusea, it was the residence of the Lords of Gruuthuse. Converted into a museum in 1955, the museum holds an array of objects depicting life between the 15th and 19th century, including furniture, kitchen equipment, silverware, tapestries, lace, ceramics, glassware, weaponry, music- and measuring-instruments, and more. Its most noteworthy room is the Room of Honour and contains tapestries, an impressive fire-place and richly decorated timber. The Brugge-musea entrance fees cover this and the next two museums.

Brangwyn Museum-Arentshuis – Dijver 16.

The first floor of this 18th century townhouse/museum is dedicated to the works of Bruges-British artist Frank Brangwyn (1867-1956). He was known for his realistic paintings and watercolours depicting the hard world of the docks and factories of the late 19th and early 20th centuries. Among his many other talents was furniture making and tapestries.

Exit the front of the museums onto Dijver. This section of the canal is called Den Dijver. The street was created from sediment of the Reie River. Turn right along one of Bruges' busiest thoroughfares. If you are interested in a boat ride, cross the street to the canal side to the promenade. Immediately in front of you is the Gruuthuse. At the corner of Dijver and Nieuuwstraat is one of the docks available for canal tours.

If you don't want a boat ride, stay on the same side of the street for the Groeninge Museum.

The Groeninge Museum – Dijver 12

Built on the site of a former Eeckhout Abbey, the Groeninge Museum is on the right at the corner of Dijver and Groening. It's known as the Bruges Museum of Fine Arts with works dating back to the 16th century. Best known are the Flemish Primitives by Jan van Eyck and Hans Memling. The museum also contains a unique collection of works by Flemish expressionists. The Groeninge is part of the Bruggemusea.

Cross over Dijver to the promenade along the canal. A few hundred metres further down at the base of the next bridge at Wollestraat is another boat dock—De Meulemeester. Alongside the Orangerie Hotel, it can be accessed by crossing the bridge and turning left at Kartuizerinnenstraat.

The Bridge of Saint Jan Nepomuc

This bridge at Wollestraat is recognizable because of the large statue in its centre. The first bridge was built in 1357, but the present was erected in 1859. The figure is that of the archbishop of Prague, Johannes Nepomusenus who was born in Bruges and martyred in 1393 by being thrown into the Moldau.

The Orangerie of the Watervliet Court – Kartuizerinnenstraat 10

This building lies across the bridge and backs up to the Den Dijver Canal. It is a former convent for the Sisters Karthuizerinnen, dating back to the 15th century. The convent is now a hotel.

Walk across Wollestraat through the archway.

Perez de Malvenda

This courtyard is entry to the 15th century mayor's house "Perez de Malvenda". In those days the Holy Blood was kept here. Since then, the entire building has been modernized but it has retained its best feature, which is a terrace that looks back at the Rozenhoedkaai. Today it's also home to the entirely Belgian product shop 2Be.

Cross back over the bridge and continue down the promenade to the fourth dock, which is just ahead at another of Bruges' most photographed and painted scenes at Rozenhoedkaai. That dock is the Coudenys.

Rozenhoedkaai

The canal takes a sharp turn at an area called the Rozenhoedkaai. Rozenhoedkaai is probably the most photographed spot in all of Bruges and is a favourite spot for artists.

From here, you get a great view of the bend in the canal with the Belfry in the background. The name comes from the term zoutendijk meaning "dike of the salt".

Continue and turn left into down Huidenvettersplein into what looks like a courtyard.

Huidenvettersplein

The street is known for its long standing pubs and restaurants as well as being home to the 17th-century Tanners' Guildhouse, the Ambachtshuis der Huidevetters. Located at Number 10, the magnificent house is now a hotel and restaurant. On a pillar in the centre of the courtyard, you will see two lions that protect the tanner's coat of arms.

Continue right around the corner and you will see the fifth and final boat dock for tours at Michielssens, which is directly behind the Burg. Don't go over the bridge in front of you yet. Turn right where you will find the open-air Fish Market.

Fish Market (Vismarkt)

There has been a Fish Market at this location for centuries. The covered market you see now was erected in 1820. If you are there between 6am-1pm, you will still witness the fishmongers selling their seafood. Accompanying them these days are a host of craftspeople selling their handmade souvenirs and even some paintings.

Turn back towards the canal and turn right for a short detour along Steen-houwersdijk-Groenerei. Here you will see the two oldest bridges in Bruges.

Meebrug and Peerdebrug Bridges

These two bridges on this narrow and picturesque section of the canal are the city's oldest. Peerdeburg or Horse Bridge used to be wooden but was re-placed by stone in the 17th century. Meeburg was built in 1390. You'll notice another almshouse just across the street at Groeneri 8. Now restored, The Pelican was built in 1708.

Turn back around and head back towards the Fish Market and cross over the bridge along the partly covered Blinde Ezelstraat.

Blinde Ezelstraat

This narrow cobbled street's name means "Blind Donkey Street" because donkeys used to be blindfolded as they came through the area. It is flanked on both sides by the Law Courts, Old Recorder's Office and the City Hall. What you'll notice most is the gilded bridge at the far end. In the archway near the end of the street is a relief depicting the Spanish grandparents of Emperor Charles— Ferdinand of Aragon and Isabelle of Castile.

Pass under the bridge and enter the Burg.

The Burg

The Burg first came into being in the 11th century when a fortress was erected here by Count Baldwin I to thwart Norman invaders. When you enter the Burg, you are surrounded by history. To your immediate right is the Old Recorder's House or Oude Griffie (Burg 11a). Also referred to as Liberty of Bruges, it was built in 1534 and is recognizable because of its own somewhat gilded façade.

To this building's right is the Old Country House the Bruge Vrije (Burg 11). Over the centuries the building has had various uses. First constructed in 1525, it was used as a palace of the region, converting to a court in 1725 and more recently as a tourism office. The ornate structure now houses the city's archives.

To your immediate left is City Hall (Burg 12). Decorated with statues of knights, it was constructed in 1376 and is one of the oldest gothic city halls in the Low Country. You'll be impressed by the Gothic Hall and its beautiful wooden ceiling and 19th-century wall paintings. Many works of art and documents showing the city's opulent history are exhibited in this room. The building is another Bruggemuseum. Directly across the courtyard and to the right is the Crown Plaza Hotel (Burg 10). It's notable because it is built on the site of St Donaas Cathedral, which was destroyed by Napoleon in 1799. The remains of the Romanesque choir gallery of the 1,000-year-old church have been incorporated into the lower levels of the hotel.

In the far left corner of the Burg is one of Bruges' most acclaimed churches – The Basilica of the Hold Blood (Burg 13), which houses the sacred relic purported to be a piece of cloth on which Christ's blood was wiped at His crucifixion. Gilded figures almost glow against the dirty stone façade of this building, parts of which date back to 1139. There are actually two churches here. At ground level is St Basil's Chapel with the Basilica occupying the upper floors. The lower chapel is quite simple, while the upper is more ornate. The "relic", which was brought to Bruges in 1150 by Count of Flanders Diederik van de Elzas, is exhibited daily.

In the park in front of the hotel, you will see a sculpture representing The Lovers, a symbolic work of art referring to the numerous young couples who come to the City Hall to be married.

As you exit the Church of the Blood, look left. At the corner of Breidelstraat and the Burg is a large stone building, which is the Baroque Deanery (Burg 3) or Provost House. Built in 1663, it used to belong to the St Donaas Cathedral.

Turn left on Breidelstraat and continue through the gauntlet of shops to the Markt.

The Market Square (Grote Markt)

While this was not originally the city centre, it is now considered the heart of Bruges. The large plaza covers almost a hectare and is a gathering place for all. It's dominated by the iconic Belfry and Market Hall at the southern end while a statue of Jan Breydel and Pieter de Coninck, two heroes of the Battle of the Spurs, sits at the north.

For centuries, this open plaza was the site of open-air stalls by the dozens and was the centre of economic, political and social life. In 1995, the Markt was renovated and traffic moved out to allow more people to enjoy it. Horse carriage rides leave from the centre and there is a huge selection of restaurants on the streets surrounding the Markt.

The original Belfry was destroyed by fire in 1280 and rebuilt in 1300 entirely of brick. From the second half of the 15th century, guardsmen would take their post in the tower and keep watch over the city. The view is incredible but bear in mind that you have to climb 366 steps before you will have a chance to enjoy it. Watch your timing, too. The tower contains the Bruges Carillon. Renowned for its range, it consists of 47 bells of various sizes and plays regularly. In fact, the city still employs a full time bell ringer.

The statue of Mary with Jesus above the archway entrance to the courtyard is just one of 600 statues of the Virgin scattered around the city. Tradition has it that in May each of them receives a garland. In the inner courtyard is another or the Bruggemusea offerings.

To the right of the Grote Markt is the Provincial Court, which was rebuilt for the fourth time in 1887. The Post Office occupies the corner where Breidelstraat leads into the square.

If you are facing the Markt from the Belfry, take a hard left on Hallestraat, which runs alongside the Market Hall. Turn right at the end of the street on Oude Burg. This route will get you out of a lot of traffic and eventually will take you along the rear of St John's Hospital. On the right is a small square called Simon Stevinplein. Simon Stevin, after whom this is named, is famous for introducing decimal fractions to the world.

You will end up behind St Saviour's Cathedral.

St Saviour's Cathedral (St-Salvatorskathedraal)

The St Saviour's Cathedral is the city's oldest parish church. Originally begun in the 9th century, the vast amount of construction took place between the 12th and 15th centuries. It was originally known as St Saviour's Church but was given the designation of "cathedral" after Saint Donaas Cathedral was destroyed.

The church contains a lot of artwork that was originally in St Donaas. Much of the most important artwork is now in the Cathedral's Treasury, which has a separate entrance. It includes paintings by, among others, Dirk Bouts and Hugo van der Goes, and manuscripts, copper memorial plaques and silver and gold artefacts.

Facing Steenstraat, turn left and continue down Zuidzandstraat and you will find yourself at t'Zand. Turn left here and you'll see a rust-coloured building on the left that looks like it is made of wooden planks. That is the Concertgebouw.

Concert Building (Concertgebouw) – 'T Zand 34

This concert hall was completed as part of Bruges' "European City of Culture of 2002" project. Although a bit odd to look at at first, it's an engineering marvel and is known for its acoustics. Designed by architects, Paul Robbrecht and Hilde Daem, it seats 1,300 and features classical music, jazz, musical theatre and visual art performances.

You'll also notice the so-called "Lantern Tower", which is slightly separated from the main building. Inside the tower is a chamber music hall that seats 300. The prices for performances at the hall start at €10.

There is also a Tourism Office located at the hall.

*Turn left out of the concert hall and the road will merge into Buiten Begijnenvest, which will take you back to the train station.*musical theatre and visual art performances.

– Walk II –
From Markt Square

This second walk covers many of the important Bruges landmarks not covered in the first walk. It is equally significant, but has the added bonus of travelling through some of the more quiet and scenic neighbourhoods not covered in the previous walk.

We start in Markt Square.

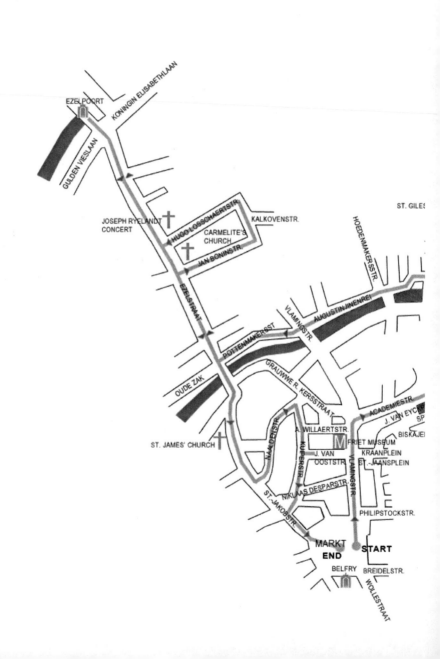

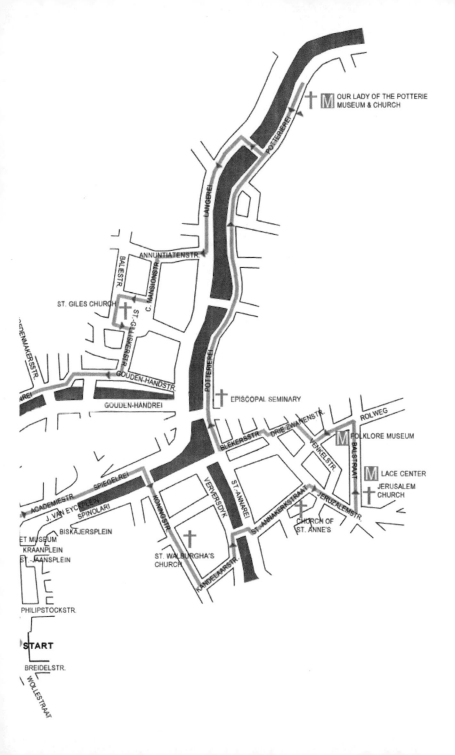

The Market Square (Grote Markt) – Grand Place

Now considered the heart of Bruges, Grote Markt was not originally the city centre. That honour belongs to the Burg, which is located down Breidelstraat immediately to the right of the Markt as you face away from the Belfry. The Belfry and Market Hall were built of brick in 1300 after fires destroyed two previous wooden bell towers. The Belfry is now part of the Bruggemusea system, which connects 16 museums throughout the city in a network where each is based on the theme of the location. You can climb the 366 steps to the top of the tower for an amazing view of the whole city as well as a close peak at Bruges Carillon, renowned for its 47 bells of various sizes.

If you are going to climb, do it now because you'll likely be too tired when you return from your walk.

As you head out across the Markt Square, you'll pass the ornate Provincial Court on your right, which was rebuilt for the fourth time in 1887. The Post Office occupies the corner where Breidelstraat leads into the square.

Straight in front of you is a large statue of two men. They are Jan Breydel and Pieter de Coninck, two heroes of the Battle of the Spurs (so named because the gilded spurs of the slain French knights were taken as war trophies during the July 11, 1302 battle.). There is a row of colourful buildings, which are mostly restaurants, directly in front of you. Take the street to the right called Vlamingstraat.

Two streets up on Vlamingstraat you will see the Royal City Theatre.

Royal City Theatre – Vlamingstraat 29

The Royal City Theatre was built in 1869 and is one of the best preserved theatre buildings in Europe. Recently restored, it is used regularly by the Bruges Culture Centre as the site for a variety of performances. The elegant neo-Renaissance façade conceals a majestic auditorium and an eclectically decorated foyer. In front of the theatre is a statue of a flute playing Papageno, the bird seller from Mozart's opera The Magic Flute.

Next door the ornate historic building houses something very, very contemporary, the Friet Museum.

Friet Museum – Vlamingstraat 33

A museum for fried potatoes? But of course! The Belgians maintain that it was they and not the French who first started frying up potato strips. Collector Eddy Van Belle created the Friet Museum in tribute to "all things fries". Van Belle also owns the Choco-Story and Lamp Museums. Among the enlightenments here: fries are best if they are fried twice. Belgians take their chips so seriously that there is even a Union of Potato Fryers and a Belgian Fryers' Day. Week of the Friet is in November!

The Fry Museum is housed in an historic building that is the last remaining of what was a trio of Italian merchant lodges representing the states of Florence, Venice and Genoa. (To learn more about this and other museums in Bruges, go to the Museums section at the back of the book.)

Next door:

House of Ter Beurze – Vlamingstraat 35

Sometimes referred to as Stock Exchange Square, Jacob van der Buerse built this house in 1423 and through those arched wooden doors is where he conceived the notion bourse or Beurs-Purse, or "stock exchange" as we know it. The KBC Bank is housed there now, so for centuries House of Ter Beurze has been a hub of locals and foreigners talking business and changing money.

When you are finished, double back a few metres and turn left on Academiestraat. This will bring you to the Jan Van Eyckplei Plaza. The body of water in front of you used to be the main commercial harbour for Bruges, the Spiegelrei Canal. To the left is the Old Toll House.

Old Toll House – Jan Van Eyckplein 2

As the name suggests, this red-doored Old Toll House was the place where tolls were levied on the goods brought in by ship from the outer ports of Bruges. Built in 1477, it was recently restored and is now a provincial information office.

Look to the left of the Toll House.

Pijnderhuisje – Jan Van Eyckplein 1

This is the narrowest building in Bruges. The figures on the façade easily display where the name comes from. The house was built by a pijnder or "docker". Pijnders were hired to unload ships.

Walk across the street to the statue in the square in front of you.

The Statue of Jan Van Eyck

The statue of Jan Van Eyck overlooks the Spiegelrei Canal, which was at one point the main harbour of Bruges. Van Eyck was an acclaimed Flemish painter, considered the best-known painter in Northern Europe in the 15th century and an innovator in oil painting techniques. He died in Bruges in 1441.

The building directly in front of the statue with the tower, opposite the canal, is the Burgher's Lodge.

Burghers' Lodge (Poortersloge) – Academiestraat 14

With its towering spire, the impressive Burghers' Lodge reflects the notoriety of the well-to-do Bruges burghers and foreign merchants who met here in a private club beginning in the 15th century. Notice the Bruges Bear in the façade, which keeps an eye on the street. Legend has it the first Count of Flanders, Baldwin with the Iron Arm, slew an aggressive bear in the woods of Beerman and to commemorate the deed, he formed the Order of the White

Bear. The bear and the lion are now the official bearers of the Bruges' coat of arms. During the 1900s, the knightly joust association De Witte Beer ("the white beer") was located in Burgher's Lodge. This is now where the state archives are stored.

Walk along the left side of the Spriegelrei and you will pass several buildings, including a hotel that used to be the receiving houses for goods. The lower levels are still massive storage areas, which are now often unused. Cross over the first bridge on the right and continue straight down Koningstraat. On the left is St Walburgha's Church.

St Walburgha's Church

The Baroque St Walburgha's Church (Sint-Walburgakerk) is tucked in the left side of Koningstraat. Built in about 1619 by the Jesuit Pieter Huyssensof, it was designed as a replica of the Gesù Church in Rome. St Walburgha's was originally attached to a Jesuit convent and dedicated to St Francis Xavier, whose statue is in a niche above the entrance. Deconsecrated in the French Revolution, the Saint-Walburgaparish took over running the church. It was rededicated in 1802. St Walburgha's contains a marble communion bench, high altar and pulpit. In the summer, the church is open to the public every evening. (To learn more about this and other churches in Bruges, go to the Churches section at the back of this book.)

When you leave the church, turn left and then left again onto Kandelaastraat. This street will take you to Verversdijik, which runs along the canal. Turn left on Verversdijik and then turn right across the bridge. You'll be entering the St Anne Quarter. Bear right and then straight down St Annakerkstraat.

Church of St Anne's – St-Annaplein

Don't let the simple exterior fool you. Walk inside this church and you will find that the Baroque interior is one of Bruges' most impressive. The most noteworthy feature is its marble rood loft created in 1626 by H. van Mildert. The present Church of St Anne's was consecrated in 1624. It took the place of an earlier gothic church that was destroyed by vandals in 1581. The acclaimed Bruges poet Guido Gazelle was baptized in St Anne's.

Turn right out of the front of St Anne's and go right on Jeruzalemstraat for two streets, to the intersection with Balstraat. This is a fairly large intersection for this neighbourhood and you will see Jerusalem Church on the left on the corner in front of you.

Jerusalem Church – Peperstraat 3

Originally built in the 15th Century as the family chapel for wealthy merchant Anselmus Adornes and his wife, the couple are now entombed in the centre of the church. Adornes was a noted traveller and Jerusalem Church was built according to the plans of the Holy Sepulchre in Jerusalem after he visited the city. In addition to the tombs, the church contains some incredible stained glass windows and has been virtually unchanged over the centuries.

In the same complex is the Lace Centre.

Lace Centre (Kantcentrum) – Peperstraat 3a

The Lace Centre is part museum, part school and part lace supply shop. As you enter past the church, on the left there is a museum section showing various styles of lace dating back centuries. Lace in Bruges can be traced to 1717 when the Sisters Apostoline set up a lace school in Ganzestraat. The non-profit Kantcentrum was founded in 1970 to encourage the art to continue. A large room at the back of the centre usually has several practitioners doing demonstrations and you'll be amazed to see the skill as they weave their spindles of thread around patterns outlined in pins on pillows. A shop in the complex sells church souvenirs as well as lace-making materials.

Exiting Jerusalem Church, go right on Balstraat to the next corner and the Folklore Museum.

Folklore Museum – Balstraat 43.

Located in eight whitewashed 17th-century almshouses belonging to the

Bruges cobblers' guild, the Folklore Museum has a large number of historic objects depicting days long since gone. There are examples of a historic classroom, cobbler's and hatter's workshops, a grocery, a Flemish living room, an old kitchen, a confectioner's, an old chemist and even an inn called De Zwarte Kat ("The Black Cat"). If you are there on Thursday afternoon, enjoy the fresh sweets they make from traditional recipes.

Turn left at the corner of Balstraat and Rolweg. After two streets, turn right on Jerusalemstraat. Go two streets and turn left on Blekersstraat. Café Vlissinghe will be on your left.

Café Vlissinghe - Blekersstraat 2

Time for a break, right? Continuously in operation for almost 500 years, Café Vlissinghe is Bruges' oldest pub. For centuries, the quaint establishment was "the" place for merchants and seamen to come during the city's heyday as a port. The décor hasn't changed much over the centuries. It is even still heated by an old stove. There is a beer garden at the rear to be enjoyed during the summer. (The café is also featured on Walk V – Historic Beer.)

When you come out of Café Vlissinghe, go left and when you reach the canal, turn right on Potterieri. The canal will be on your left and you should walk several hundred metres, passing two bridges until you see the Episcopal Seminary on your right.

Episcopal Seminary (Bisschoppelijk Seminarie) - Potterieri 72

Now a seminary with more than 100 students training to be Catholic priests, the Episcopal Seminary was once a Cistercian abbey called "Ter Duinen". The Monks fled after the French revolution and over the centuries it served as military hospital, a military depot and even a grammar school before becoming the Great Seminary in 1833. The brick complex also includes an impressive 18th-century church and a lovely orchard. Don't be surprised to find cows grazing in the field.

Our Lady of the Potterie Museum and Church – Potterieri 79

The Baroque Our Lady of the Potterie Museum and its hospital complex were built in the 13th century to service pilgrims and the sick. The older buildings now house a museum while a residential facility for the elderly occupies the newer buildings. The museum contains an impressive collection of works of art, including objects related to healthcare, worship and the monastery. The museum is part of the Bruggemusea.

Cross back over Potterieri and turn left, walking with the canal on your right and cross the footbridge. Travel down Langerei two streets, turning right on Annuntiatenstraat. At the next street, turn left on Collaert Mansionstraat. You are in the neighbourhood of St Giles and the church in front of you is its namesake. The neighbourhood is known for being an artists' quarter.

St Giles – Gillisker

St Giles church sits in the centre of a square and the neighbourhood grew up around it. The entrance is on the side opposite from where you enter the square. The church was originally founded in 1240 as a chapel, but quickly became a parish church. It continued to expand throughout the 15th century.

The organ is considered one of the best in the city and there are also a number of significant paintings inside, including four by Brugean painter Jan Garemijn depicting the history of the "Trinitarian" brotherhood. Hans Memling, Pierter Pourbus and Lanceloot Blondeel are among those believed buried in the churchyard.

Go round to the left of the church when you exit and turn right on St Gilliskerkstraat. The road will end at the canal. Turn right on Gouden-handstraat. Follow the canal past four bridges, turning right at the fifth onto Elzelstraat. Within two streets you will see another church on your right.

Carmelite's Church – Ezelstraat 28

The church takes up most of the street. Built in 1688, the Baroque church also includes a 17th century plague house in the garden. Each Sunday, you can enjoy the sounds of Gregorian Mass at this church.

Keep walking for one more street.
Joseph Ryelandt Concert – Ezelstraat 3

A former Anglican Church, this 19th-century building now serves as the Joseph Ryelandt Concert hall. It was named after the Brugean Composer Joseph Ryelandt. This building is part of the Bruges Culture Centre.

Stay right on Ezelpoort until you reach Koningin Elisabethlaan and cross over.

Ezelpoort

Also known as Donkey Gate or the sometimes more entertaining Ass's Gate, Ezelpoort is probably the less visited of all the gates because it's located more in the neighbourhoods of Bruges than the tourism centre. The gate has been fully restored and the grounds include a moat. Traffic has diverted around the structure and the gate now serves as a foot and bicycle path.

There are two towers with 360-degree windows at the top and a room with a small centre tower in between. The bell at the top is decorative now, but when Ezelpoort was a functional entrance to the city, the bell would be rung to signal to people in the area that the gate was about to close. The centre gateway is arched. (All of the city gates are included in Walk III.)

When you have finished visiting the gate, turn around and head back down Ezelpoort, crossing over the canal and continuing onto St Jakobstraat.

St James's Church

St James's Church was founded as a branch of St Saviour's Church in about 1420 during a time of expansion in the city and was built through funds donated by the Duke of Burgundy. The neighbourhood around it grew to include more of the city's upper crust, including businessmen and foreign dignitaries, and the church benefited from the money. It has several chapels within and is noted for its extensive collection of artwork. There are over 80 paintings inside, including a celebrated depiction of the legend of St Lucy and a few important works by Pieter Pourbus.

St James's oak pulpit is particularly noteworthy for its detailed carvings. It's supported by four figures that represent the known continents of that period: Asia, Africa, America and Europe. Also notice the Chapel of Ferry de Gros, which contains the mausoleum of Ferry de Gros who was the treasurer of the Order of the Golden Fleece. (The Order was an order of knights founded in 1430 by Duke Philip the Good of Flanders.)

After visiting St James, turn left on Boterhuis and then right on Naaldenstraat or "Needle Street". On the corner is the Lodge of Lucca.

Lodge of Lucca – Naaldenstraat 30

Established in 1400, Lodge of Lucca was the home of the merchants and bakers from Lucca. The Merchants specialized in the import of luxurious textiles such as velvet and gold brocade. The bankers supporting them dominated the capital market in Bruges during the 15th century.

Bladelin Court – Naaldenstraat 19.

Opposite the Lodge is Bladelin Court. The home was built circa 1435 by Pieter Bladelin, treasurer of the Order of the Golden Fleece. The walls surrounding the charming inner garden show impressive stone medallions representing portraits of the former inhabitants. In the 19th century the priest Leon de Foere established a lace school here.

Go round the corner onto Kuiperstraat and on the right is the City Library.

City Library de Beikorf – Kuiperstraat 3

The City Library de Beikorf (meaning "beehive"), also called Hoofdbibliotheek, is a decorative slim stone building with the coat of arms of the rulers of Luxembourg and is easy to spot. The building was originally a place where importers had to pay duties on their goods.

Keep heading down Kuiperstraat and you will pass the rear of the Royal City Theatre and eventually cross over Niklass Desparstraat. Bear left and cut through the pedestrian zone at Eiermarkt. You will end up back in the Markt Square.

De Gouden Meermin – Markt 31

On the north side of the Markt, notice De Gouden Meermin or "the Golden Basket", which can be seen in the gables above the 17th-century house. They pay tribute to the tillers and fishmongers who had stands in Markt Square until 1745.

In 1995, the Markt was renovated and traffic moved out to allow more people to enjoy it. Horse carriage rides leave from the centre now and there is a huge selection of restaurants on the streets surrounding the Markt.

– Walk III –
City Gates and Wind Mills

From 1297 to 1782, Bruges was a walled city. Its historic centre is still isolated from the rest of the town by canals and a ring road. For those who have already wandered the interior and want to head out for a longer hike, you can walk virtually all the way around the city. Four of the original nine city gates remain and there are also four windmills. The entire stroll can be both relaxing and invigorating.

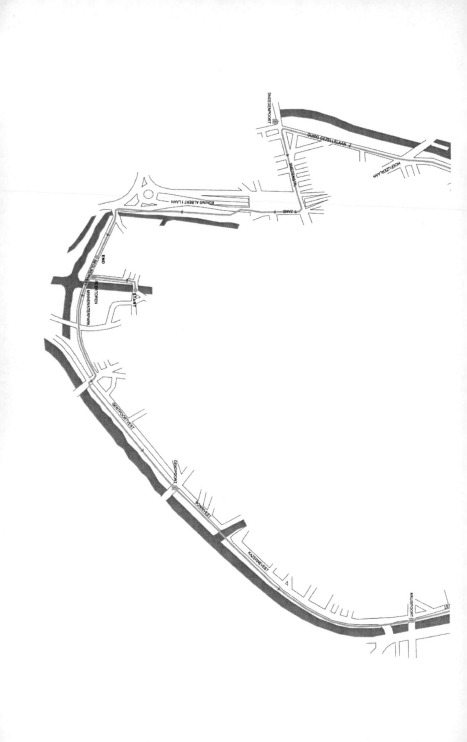

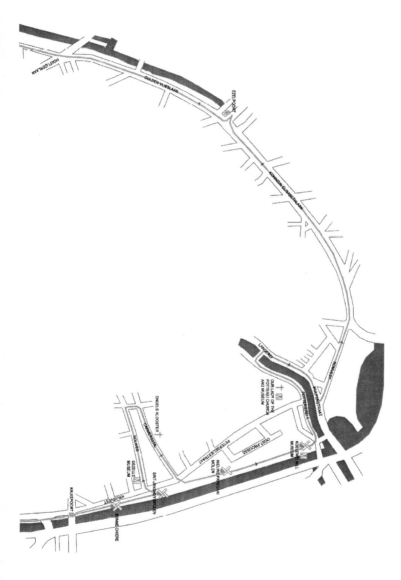

Starting point – South End of Minnewater (Lake of Love)

You'll be walking anticlockwise for the full 7km (4mi) ring around Bruges, starting from the south end of Minnewater (Lake of Love) at the corner of the tree-lined path that intersects at the corner with Begijnenvest.

The Lake of Love

The Lake of Love was the former inner harbour of Bruges: the confluence of the Reie River and the Sint-Michiels Kerkebeek. Barges transporting people from Ghent used to enter the city here after their eight-hour journey. The lake itself was created around 1200 when locks were built.

There are several stories as to why it is called the Lake of Love. Legend has it that a woman named Minna was promised to one man while loving another. She fled her father and died here on the banks where her lover later found her. He diverted the river and buried her body where the water now flows. Another fable has it that the lake is home to a "min" or water sprites who play love songs to influence couples who may find themselves wandering the area.

At the corner of the Begijnenvest and the path next to the lake, there is a three-storey brick tower next to the bridge that marks the entrance to the Lake.

Poertoren

This tower is called the Poertoren and was built in 1398. A defensive tower from the original city walls, it was used for gunpowder storage and a workshop. In fact Poer means "powder". Its twin tower used to be directly opposite on the other side of the bridge.

Cross the bridge and you may want to take a quick detour to your left through the Minnewaterpark.

Minnewaterpark.

Minnewaterpark was built in 1979 on what used to be the site of an old castle's grounds. The castle is long since gone but the porter's lodge and gardens remain. The park is the site of the annual Cactus Festival each July, which features national and international artists and musicians.

When you get back on track, follow the footpath and cross over Katelijnestraat. Then, go up to the embankment that will take you most of the way around the city.

Rampart Foot Path

This green pathway is where the Brugean Ramparts stood for almost 500 years. The canal you are now walking beside is the Bruges-Ghent Canal, which was dug out after the West Scheldt route was blockaded by the Dutch in 1604. You will notice Katelijnestraat has a bridge that crosses over the canal. That bridge is located where one of the now demolished city gates used to be. Today, Kateljnepoort is simply an ordinary swing bridge.

The street Gentpoortvest will be on your left as you stroll along the embankment but it's often obscured by trees. After a few hundred metres, you'll pass another tower. While it looks like it could be from Bruges' day as a walled city, it is not. It was actually constructed circa 1925-1926. There is no public access, but it certainly adds to the historical atmosphere.

Gentpoort

Gentpoort is the first city gate you will encounter. A sturdy brick structure with four towers, it is easy to see how the gate was built for defensive purposes. From the outside, it looks quite imposing, while the town side of the building fits more with the surrounding architecture. The gate is too narrow for modern-day traffic, so vehicles now drive around it. This makes it easy for you to take a full tour. The drawbridge that once led to the gate is also long gone, but the statue of St Adrian remains in a nook above the door. The

shrine was placed there to help protect the city from invaders.

Gentpoort was originally constructed in 1297. About 150 years later, it was rebuilt along with Kateljnepoort and Kruispoort by Jan van Oudenaarde. After Austrian Emperor Joseph II ordered the demolition of the Ramparts surrounding Bruges in 1782, the town gates for a time served as toll gates. When toll taxes were finally discontinued in the 1860s, the town saw the gates as obsolete and started to demolish them. They'd already got rid of Katelijine, Broeverie and Damspoort before historians stepped in and saved the remaining four. Gentpoort is notable because this is the gate the Germans fled through when they evacuated Bruges on September 12, 1944 as Canadian forces moved in.

In 2008, a museum was opened in the upper floor of the building where a great room runs the full length. The museum is part of Bruggemusea system which features 11 museums located in historical buildings throughout the city. Each tells the city's history from the perspective of the theme in which they fall. Gentpoort features the story of all of the gates as well as the ramparts. Hours vary per season. (For more on the Bruggemusea and other museums around Bruges, go to the Museums section in the back of this book.)

Continue on your journey along the Rampart footpath and you will soon come to the next city gate, Kruispoort.

Kruispoort

Also called Cross Gate, this gate also dates back to 1297. Traffic still flows into the city through the gate on Langestraat, but traffic coming out must go across another bridge that has been constructed just to the south. A pedestrian path and bridge run on the north side of the structure.

Because Kruispoort was rebuilt in 1402 by the same architect as Gentpoort, it looks very similar with the imposing fortress-like outer walls and more castle-like appearance on the city-side. But there is something that sets it apart from the other remaining gates. It was built of white sand lime bricks and although reconstructed several times, it has been meticulously restored to its original appearance.

It is, however, missing its original gates, which have not been needed for centuries. The building contains five vaults that now house some of the architectural features that used to be on the exterior. A nook above the gate on the town side of Kruispoort features a crucifix.

Kruispoort holds the distinction of being the path the Germans took when they left on October 19, 1918.

From Kruispoort, you can see four windmills ahead. At one point, Bruges had more than 29 mills. Most were grain mills although there were some water mills and a few oil mills. These four are the only ones to remain.

Bonne Chiere

This first windmill is called Bonne Chiere which refers to "the Good Life". It's actually a replacement mill for the original Bonne Chiere. Built in 1888 in East Flanders in the town of Olsene, it was brought to Bruges and reconstructed in 1911. Sitting on brick pillars, the wooden silt mill originally had three mill stones. This mill is no longer in use.

St John's House Mill (Sint-Janshuysmolen)

Immediately past Bonne Chiere is the Sint-Janshuysmolen. St John's House Mill was built in 1770 and is the oldest of the mills still standing, and for that matter, still working. Constructed by a group of 26 bakers, it still functions as an active grain mill, as well as a museum. Combined with the Koelewei Mill further up the embankment, the two make up what is called the Bruggemuseum-Molens (or the Mill Museum).

The rectangular wooden body of the mill is supported by a trestle consisting of the trunks of eight trees. It's designed to rotate around a main post so that the wings will face the wind. It's only open from May until late September, but it includes an interesting exhibit. Brave souls can also climb a steep, narrow staircase to the top of the main wheelhouse.

The mill stands on a mound that dates back to 1297 and it is on the same site where another mill that serviced the St John's Hospital had stood previously. That mill was destroyed by wind in 1744.

Before you continue to the other mills, it may be time for another detour. Walk directly down the hill towards the area where you see two fenced-in green fields. On the left is a row of white buildings. Cross over Kruisvest and continue directly up Rolweig. on your right is the wall to the grounds for the Saint Sebastian Archer's Guild, which you'll see in a few minutes.

Guido Gezelle Museum – Rolweg 64

The building on the left is the Guido Gezelle Museum, birthplace of the famous 19th-century Flemish poet. Today it is a literary museum with a peaceful garden. Further details are included in the Museums section of this guide.

At the end of the stone wall surrounding the archer's guild, turn right on Speelmannstraat and right again on Carmersstraat.

English Convent (Engels Klooster) – Carmersstraat 85

On the left you will see an imposing domed church and its walls. The church was built between 1736 and 1739, but the convent has been here since 1629. It was founded as a haven for English nuns and monks who were escaping persecution in Britain when King Henry VIII banned Catholicism.

The convent was expanded in the 18th century at which time the domed church was constructed, but the community had to flee when French rule began in 1794. The convent was sold, but the nuns were able to purchase it in 1804 and turn it into a school. Services are still held so wander inside and have a look at the beautiful interior. The one-aisled church is richly decorated with a main altar made of 23 different marble pieces.

Since the boarding school it once housed has been closed, the convent is now open for overnight guests and meditation, meetings, conferences, courses, study or silent days. (For more on the Churches of Bruges, refer to the Churches section at the back of this book.)

Continue down the street to the red-bricked wall and large building at no. 174.

Saint Sebastian's Archer Guild – Carmersstraat 174

The Saint Sebastian Archer's Guild dates back to the Middle Ages, when the group was part of the local militia. The highly respected guild used their skills with the long bow during the crusades and in return were allowed to use the Jerusalem crucifix in their coat of arms. The guild moved into this complex in 1573 and has had its share of illustrious guests.

The exiled English King Charles II and his brother Henry Stuart, Duke of Gloucester lived here from 1656-1659 and became members of the guild. Paintings of the royal patrons are displayed on the walls of the royal hall and to this day, if the British Royal family travels to Bruges, they pay a visit here in tribute to the guild's role in housing and protecting Charles.

A vaulted gallery contains a treasure trove of paintings and archives chronicling the guild's rich history. The guild hall is constructed of brick and is recognizable by its tower. Inside, you will find that each floor has a different shape, ranging from round to square to octagonal. In addition to the gallery, the building contains an orchestra room and theatre.

It is largely used for recreational purposes now, but still houses important documents in its record office.

Continue down Carmersstraat and cross over Kruisvest again and travel up the embankment, turning left.

De Nieuwe Papegaai Molen

The next mill is a former oil mill called De Nieuwe Papegaai. Originally built in the 18th century in Beveren-Ijzer where it was called Hoge Seinemolen or "High Signal Mill", it was reconstructed here in 1970 on the former site of an old stone mill. The wooden structure stands on a closed brick mill house and has a whimsical parrot on its weather vane.

The Barges

Keeping walking along the rampart and you will pass two wooden barges that have been converted into homes—the Taranta and the Rio Clara. Both are quite old and if you're lucky, in the summer, you may be able to even meet the owners who reside there. The Rio Clara was built in 1889.

Koelewei Mill

Next on the walk is the Koelewei Mill, which has been standing since 1765 and is still going strong as an active mill in the summer months. Along with the Sint-Janshuis Mill, Koelewei (which means "cool meadow") makes up the Bruggemuseum-Molens (or the Mill Museum). The Mill was moved from its original location to its current spot near the Dam Gate of Bruges. Visitors are allowed to climb to the top of the millhouse, and can see it in operation as long as they visit during the spring and summer months when it is fully functional.

Damspoort

Just ahead are the busy road Potterieri and the Damsport entrance to the city. Here is where you can see the city's biggest locks and the zone around it is fairly industrial. You may even see some commercial vessels docked here.

This is where you would catch a barge for a day trip to the nearby city of Damme. Damsport used to be the site of yet another of the defunct city gates, which was built in 1621. This is where the ocean-going vessels would pass through the Damse Vaart Canal and into the city.

At one time Napoleon Bonaparte had great plans to link this area by canal to Antwerp, where he hoped to create a naval base. Bonaparte even had Spanish prisoners working on it before Belgium gained independence.

Turn left on Potterieri and head south with the Potterieri on your left.

Our Lady of the Potterie Museum and Church – Potterie 79

The baroque church and its hospital complex were built in the 13th century to service pilgrims and the sick. The older buildings now house a museum while a residential facility for the elderly occupies the newer buildings. The impressive collection museum includes works of art as well as objects related to healthcare, worship and the monastery. The museum is part of the Bruggemusea.

Episcopal Seminary (Bisschoppelijk Seminarie) – Potterie 72

Right next door is the Episcopal Seminary. Now an operational seminary with more than 100 students, this was once a former Cistercian abbey called Ter Duinen. It has served in many capacities over the centuries, including a military installation. The huge brick complex also includes an impressive 18th-century church.

Have a peak at the Seminary and then cross the street to turn right across the small wooden footbridge. Turn left on Langerei and then right on Julius ed Mauritis Sabbestraat. This will take you back to the inner ring road, Komvest. Cross over and go left.

This neighbourhood has a distinctly residential feel. The shops and homes are actually built over the top of the canal that runs underneath. When Bruges anticipated expansion a century or so ago, this area was filled in to accommodate all of the anticipated growth that never took place.

Komvest changes name to Koningin Elisabethlaan but stay the course. Almost immediately you will see Ezelpoort.

Ezelpoort

Ezelpoort is known as Donkey Gate or the sometimes more entertaining Ass's Gate. This gate is probably the least visited of all the gates because by now you have no doubt noticed that you are a bit off the beaten path and in a more suburban area.

Still, Ezelpoort is in great shape, having been fully restored. The grounds are very nice and include a moat. Traffic has diverted around the structure and the gate now serves as a foot and bicycle path.

There are two towers with 360-degree windows at the top and a room with a small centre tower in between. The bell at the top is decorative now, but when Ezelpoort was a functional entrance to the city the bell would be rung to signal to people in the area that the gate was about to close. The centre gateway is arched.

When leaving Elzepoort, continue along with the canal to your right.

You'll pass over Kanel de Stouteln and the busy thoroughfare at Bloedport—so named because until the 16th century this was the place healers would come to dump the blood from their daily bloodlettings. The pit is still there. You'll then find yourself walking through one of Bruges' favourite park areas, lined with trees that include oak, chestnut and lime. You'll encounter joggers, dog walkers and those who just want to enjoy a bit of nature.

Smeedenpoort

At the end of the park you will find the last remaining city gate—Smeedenpoort or "Blacksmith's Gate". Originally built in 1367, it has undergone several renovations, the most recent in 2008-2009. As with the other gates, the exterior has the imposing fortress-like appearance but Smeedenpoort is unique in that the interior has a more cottage style. Traffic still flows through the gate with opposite directions dictated by a red light on either side. There are also pedestrian walkways on both sides.

An opening above the gate once contained a bronze replica of the head of the ill-fated traitor Francois vander Straeten from Ghent. Vander Straeten opened the gate to French invaders in the 17th century and was hung at Smeedenpoort for his deed.

The building also has a bell at the top that would ring to announce when the gate would be closing.

Proud of yourself? You've almost circumnavigated the whole city. You are now just a few hundred metres from the train station again. Reward yourself by turning left on Smeedenstraat and find a café to sit and rest your tired feet. There are several along this area, or, if you choose, go a few more streets to the public parking area at 't Zand where the square is lined with restaurants and cafes.

– Walk IV –
Chocolate

O nce you've tasted Belgian chocolate, there is no going back. Pure and simple, it is a truly melt-in-your-mouth pleasure. As well known as Belgium is
for chocolate, Bruges claims to be the Belgian chocolate capital. Of the 45 shops
in Bruges, the vast majority will likely have the owner there behind the counter
to tell you with pride why they feel their chocolates are the best.

Chocolate first came to Europe courtesy of the Spanish after conquistadors
discovered the Aztecs sipping on a spicy drink created from roasted cacao
beans. The newcomers tossed in a little sugar to make it more palatable and
brought it back to share with the royal courts. Initially used for medicinal
purposes, this newfound drink was so precious that only the nobility and
their friends could partake of it. Eventually it evolved into the delicacy we
enjoy today.

Pure chocolate consists of nothing but cocoa powder, cocoa butter and sugar. It melts very easily. The temperature at which it is cooled affects how shiny
the final product appears, as well as how sweet it will taste.

Because there are no preservatives... eat up! You wouldn't want it to melt
or go off! Chocolatiers in Bruges are very competitive and carefully guard the
secrets behind their recipes and techniques.

So seriously do Brugeans take their place in the chocolate world that chocolate dominates dessert menus. Virtually every restaurant serves hot chocolate—often in some of the most creative manners you will ever see. There
is even a Chocolate Festival each April or May in which all sorts of tastings
take place as well as chocolate sculpting and chocolate painting! Only local
chocolatiers are allowed to participate.

Bruges also has an official city chocolate—the Bruges Swan or Brugsch
Swaentje, which is sold in shops that are members of the Bruges Chocolate
Guild. The exact recipe remains a secret, but among the key ingredients are
almond paste, gruut (a local type of spiced flour) and kletskoppen (a local
biscuit).

This walk is designed to take you to places with unique offerings to try.
Remember to pace yourself as you go on this walk! The best place to start
is a location that will help you understand a bit more about what you are
experiencing—the Chocolate Museum. The Choco-Story is located in the St
Jansplein plaza on the corner of St Jansstraat and Wijnzakstraat.

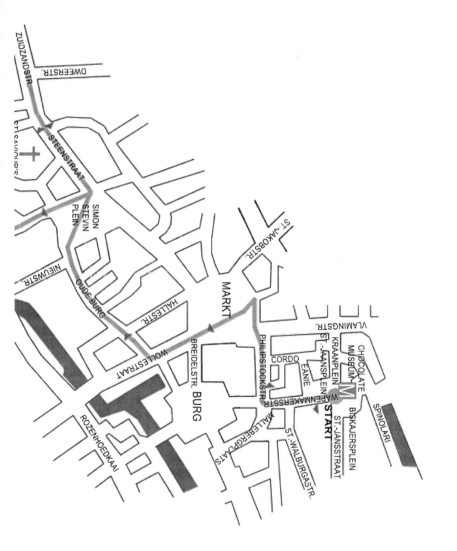

Choco-Story

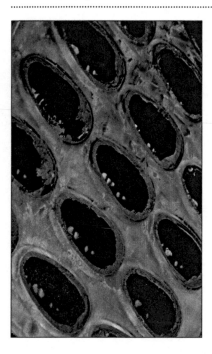

Wijnzakstraat 2 (St Jansplein)
Phone: 32 50 61 22 37
www.choco-story.be

A stop at this museum helps you trace the history of chocolate through its 2,600-year history. Guided by a chocolate fairy, you will wander four floors filled with information about the discovery of the cacao bean and how chocolate evolved into what it is today. The museum offers a fun and educational experience and of course lets you sample.

Given the history shared here, it's only appropriate that Choco-Story is located in a beautiful 15th-century building. In addition to samples, they will give you a map that shows the location of every chocolate shop in Bruges. But stick with us and our walk!

When you exit the museum, head back towards the Burg on Wapenmaker-straat. Turn right on Philipstockstraat. Sweertvaegher will be on your right.

Sweertvaegher

Philipstockstraat 29
Phone: 32 50 33 83 67
www.sweertvaegher.be

Opened in 1933, this shop is a traditional chocolaterie. Sweertvaegher is known for its pralines, truffles, chocolate bars, figures and doopsuiker, the special Belgian sweet used at christenings. There are three other Sweertvae-gher shops across Belgium. Try the doopsuiker.

As you leave the shop, continue on Philipstockstraat, which will take you to the north side of the Markt, opposite the Belfry. Go past Vlamingstraat and turn right on Eiermarkt, which is a pedestrian area.

Dumon

Eiermarkt 6
Phone: 32 50 34 62 82
www.chocobong.com
Dumon is named after its owner and chocolatier, Stefan Dumon, who along with his wife Marie-Anne creates most of these wonderful chocolates. A true artisan, Dumon prides himself on his creativity. Some of his unique offerings include ginger-filled chocolates, chocolate cherries and Chocodips. The dips are chocolate on a stick that you put in warm milk and let the melted chocolate create a creamy hot chocolate.

There are three locations for Dumon around Bruges. You have to try the ginger chocolate here.

Head back towards the Markt and go to the opposite end of the square, to the street just to the left of the Belfry. That is Wollestraat. Van Oost will be on your left about one street down.

Van Oost

Wollestraadt 11
Phone: 32 50 33 14 54
www.chocolatiervanoost.be
A small shop, but Van Oost is worth a visit for the handmade pralines. You'll be surprised by the variety available in such a tiny shop. But pace yourself and try to limit just how many you sample! This chocolatier is a purist when it comes to creations and you can taste the pride. Try the chocolate mousse praline.

Just next door is Chocoladehuisje.

Chocoladehuisje

Wollestraat 15
Phone: 32 50 34 02 50
www.chocoladehuisjebrugge.be
This shop is entirely different from most shops you'll see. The window at Chocoladehuisje is filled with figures and masks made of chocolate and marzipan. They offer more than 60 items to choose from so making a decision could be hard. How about the chocolate-covered marzipan?

Continue down Wollestraat and turn right on Oude Burge. Five streets down, you will come to an area called Simon Stevin Plein, turn right to find The Chocolate Line.

The Chocolate Line

Simon Stevinplein 19
Phone: 32 50 34 10 90
 www.thechocolateline.be
This shop is known for its creativity. Owners Fabienne Destaercke and Dominique Persoone fancy themselves "Shock-o-latiers" combining chocolate with peas, tequila, cola, oysters, chicken—you name it. Even the displays will have you taking photographs if you aren't brave enough to sample. Step outside the box and try one of their unique offerings. It doesn't have to be extreme. Chocolate and garlic perhaps? Or perhaps the chilli-lime?

Continue across Simon Steve Plein to Steenstraat, cross the street and turn left. After about one street, on your right, on the corner of Zilverstraat and opposite St Saviour's Cathedral is a complex called Zilverpand. Go in here.

Chocolate Bar

Zilverpand 9
Phone: 32 475 66 04 06
www.bar-c.be
Ready for food? In addition to the chocolates, there is some serious food here. All chocolate related, of course. How about stewed meat with sauce made of Leffe beer and chocolate? Chocolate fondue, chocolate pancakes. There are 44 kinds of hot and cold chocolate including white hot chocolate or banana and ginger hot chocolate. Try the stew.

Double back on Steenstraat to Simon Stevnl Plein and turn right. Cross the Square to Mariastraat to find another Dumon Chocolate and then right next door, the Old Chocolate House.

The Old Chocolate House

Mariastraat 1c,
Phone: 32 50 34 01 02
www.oldchocolatehouse.com
Considered one of Bruges' better valued chocolate shops, this shop is operated by the friendly Françoise Thomaes and Barbe. Guaranteed fresh, their truffled chocolate pralines, as well as gingerbreads, biscuits, marzipan and sweets are enough to satisfy any chocoholics. Try the liqueur chocolates.

Continue walking down Mariastraat where you will walk past the Church of Our Lady. You are about to enter Chocolate Heaven. There will be several chocolate shops ahead. Pass them by and turn right into the Alley at Stoofstraat, Bruges' most narrow street.

Tsjokoreeto

Stoofstraat 4
Phone: 32 50 34 25 56
It's appropriate that the chocolate here is sinfully good. Tsjokoreeto is located on one of Bruges' most notoriously sinful streets. This was the place where Bruges' bathhouses and brothels were located almost 500 years ago. You can now take pleasure with these chocolates. Try the champagne truffles.

Exit back out the alley and turn right. On your right is the tearoom Tde Proeverij.

Tde Proeverie

Katelijnestraat 3
Phone: 32 50 33 08 87
This little tearoom will change your mind about the best way to have hot chocolate. It's served "the Belgian way". Order it and a steaming, frothy cup of hot milk arrives with a small dish of melted chocolate on top. Add the chocolate and whip cream yourself and the combination is amazing. Tde Proeverie is owned by the same

people who own Sukerbuyc Chocolates across the street so your hot chocolate comes with a few pieces as well.

When you've relaxed and enjoyed, cross over the street of Sukerbuyc.

Sukerbuyc

Katelijnestraat 5 & 6
Phone: 32 50 33 08 87
www.sukerbuyc.com
Sukerbuyc is one of only about 5 of the 45 chocolate shops that make their own blends of chocolate. It's all made right here on the premises so the smell in the shop is amazing. Chocolatier Kristoff Deryckere is a real artist and there are some unbelievable chocolate displays in the store. Sukerbuyc considers itself a "classic" shop. Just a taste will easily set it apart. They are known for their decorated chocolate boxes, topped with scenes from Bruges in white chocolate. Try a box billed with chocolate strawberries.

Turn left out of Sukerbuyc and cross back over the street. Go one street and turn right on Walstraat and then left across the cobbled square to Walpein. Begijnte 'T is on your right at the corner of Wijngaadstraat..

't Begijntje

Wijngaardstraat 16
Phone: 32 50 33 85 60
www.chocolat-begijntje.be
The building itself is as inviting as the scrumptious chocolates that waits inside. The shop has been here since 1986 and it has a reputation for offering not only high quality chocolates, but nine different types of marzipan, in addition to its own assortments of chocolate bursting with nuts, orange peel and cherries, 't Begijntje is the exclusive distributor in the region of the Café-Tasse chocolate products. You have to taste one of those enticing individually wrapped squares of chocolate.

Diagonally on the opposite corner is the appropriately named Chocolate Corner.

The Chocolate Corner

....

Wijngaardstraat 17
Phone: 32 50 34 38 98

Appropriately called the Chocolate Corner, this is a great place to end your walk. Inside this whitewashed old Flemish store, you will find some amazing unique offerings including their famous tea-flavoured pralines. The little shop offers a wide variety from which to choose and is also known for its liqueur-filled truffles. But here, if there is only one thing you could taste, it would be the tea-flavoured pralines. But since this is the last stop, feel free to indulge.

Exiting the Chocolate Corner, turn left and end your walk at the Beguinage.

Below is a list of all the chocolate shops in Bruges and their locations.

Shop	Address	Telephone (country code 32)
ArtiChoc	Geldmuntstraat 12	050 33 31 99
Bar Chocolate	Zilverpand 8	04 75 66 04 06
Chocoladehuisje	Wollestraat 15	050 34 02 50
Chocolaterie De Burg	Burg 15	050 33 52 32
Choco-Story	Wijnzakstraat 2 (St Jansplein)	050 61 22 37
De Clerck	Academiestraat 19	050 34 53 38
Depla Pol Chocolatier	Eekhoutstraat 27	050 33 49 53
Dumon Chocolatier	Walstraat 6	050 34 00 43
Dumon Chocolatier	Eiermarkt 6	050 34 62 82
Dumon Chocolatier	Simon Stevinplein II	050 33 33 60
Galler	Steenstraat 5	050 61 20 62
Godiva	Zuidzandstraat 36	050 33 28 66
Huis Sandy	St Amandsstraat 27	050 34 87 69
Lady Chocolates	Katelijnestraat 60	050 33 78 40
Leonidas	NoordZandstraat 93	050 34 42 26
Leonidas	Katelijnestraat 24	050 34 69 41
Leonidas	Steenstraat 82	050 61 22 67
Leonidas	Steenstraat 4	050 33 40 60
Marie	Langestraat 81	050 35 89 76
Moeder Babelutte	Katelijnestraat 26	050 34 75 45
Moeder Babelutte	Rozenhoedkaai 1	04 77 54 50 49
Moeder Babelutte	Wollestraat 24	050 34 83 07

Shop	Address	Telephone (country code 32)
Neuhaus	Steenstraat 66	050 33 15 30
Pralinette	Wollestraat 31b	050 34 83 83
Pralinique de Bruges	Katelijnestraat 35	050 34 37 59
Princesse	Wollestraat 16	050 33 23 42
Roose's Chocolate City	Steenstraat 47	050 33 23 30
Roose's Chocolate World	Havenstraat 1	050 34 78 60
Spegelaere	Ezelstraat 92	050 33 60 52
Stefs Chocolatier	Breidelstraat 7	050 33 25 45
Sukerbuyc	Katelijnestraat 5	050 33 08 87
Sweertvaegher	Philipstockstraat 29	050 33 83 67
Sweet Moment	Hoogstraat 47	050 49 12 32
't Begijntje	Wijngaardstraat 16	050 33 85 60
Temmerman	Zilverpand 12	050 33 16 78
The Chocolate Corner	Wijngaardstraat 17	050 34 38 98
The Chocolate Line	S. Stevinplein 19	050 34 10 90
The Old Chocolate House	Mariastraat 1C	050 34 01 02
Truffelhuisje	St Amandsstraat 3	050 34 26 57
Tsjokoreeto	Stoofstraat 4	050 34 25 56
Van Tilborgh	Noordzandstraat 1 bis	050 33 59 04
Verheecke	Katelijnestraat 22	050 34 97 47
Yves	Rozenhoedkaai 6	050 33 81 65

– Walk V –
Historic Beer

In a country known for its beers, Bruges stands out as a place to go and enjoy a brew. In fact it's not surprising that there are many who come to Bruges to partake of beer and not the city's history. It won't take long to find that beer history and Bruges' history are intertwined. This was a port after all!

Centuries ago, there were hundreds of establishments brewing their own beers and as of the early 20th century, there were still more than two dozen official breweries. Beer wagons hauled by Belgium draft horses were plentiful in the streets.

The brewing activity has died considerably, but the drinking has not. Belgium is known to have more than 400 types of beers and you can find them all here.

We'll call this a "beer walk", but if you truly hit them all it will become a "beer crawl". We start at Bruges' lone remaining brewery, De Halve Maan.

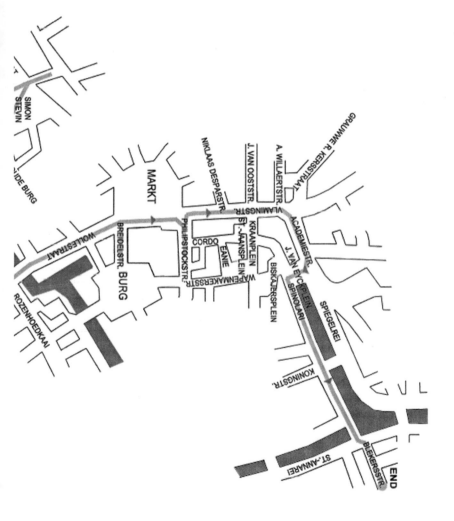

Brewery De Halve Maan

Walplein 26
Phone: 32 50 33 26 97
www.halvemaan.be

A brewery has stood on this site since the 16th century. Henry Maes took the operations over in 1856 and founded De Halve Maan or Half Moon Brewery, which is still run by his descendents. More importantly, this brewery is the only one remaining operational in the city limits. And even though it has outgrown the site, the owners say that some beer will always be brewed here just because of the building's long history.

You enter the brewery's gates and walk through a tunnel to a courtyard where the tour gathers. Buy your tickets for the hour-long tour in the restaurant. Reservations may be needed depending on the time of year.

The presentation takes you up 220 steps and offers information on the history of Bruges and its beers, so this is a great place to start your beer walk. The trip to the roof provides a fabulous panorama of the city and will whet your appetite for your drinking and walking.

You'll wind through various rooms that are no longer in use but have great history behind them. The Brewery itself has been modernized and what used to take 50 people to accomplish can now be handled by the brew master and three assistants. While the beer is brewed here, it is aged and bottled elsewhere because there isn't enough space to meet the growing demands.

The tour ends back in the restaurant. A tour ticket entitles you to a glass of their signature Brugse Zot beer, but several other varieties are available. The restaurant has a hearty menu. In case you're interested, zot means "lunatic".

Exit the Half Moon and cross the cobbled square in front of you. Walk up Walstrasse one street and turn left on Katelijnestraat. Go past the Cathedral of Our Lady. The road splits three ways just past the church. Stay in the centre and continue on Mariastraat. You'll cross Oud Burg (a street), then Simon Stevin Plein (a square), and then across Steenstraat. Mariastraat changes name to Kemelstraat.

't Brugs Beertje

Kemelstraat 5
Phone: 32 50 33 96 16
www.brugsbeertje.be

For many beer aficionados 't Brugs Beertje is a "must visit" when in Bruges. You will notice straight away something they call a "beer spirit" when you enter the building. The maze of small rooms is decorated with beer memorabilia, much of which is traced to the 300 types of Belgian beer served here, including some on draft. The waiters and bartenders are experts on each so feel free to say what sort of flavour you are looking for and they will help you sort through the expansive list.

The owners of 't Brugs Beertje promote the beer culture in Bruges and helped establish the Beer Festival. The pub features beers of the month and changes the draft beers regularly. There are also beer souvenirs available.

Exit 't Brugs Beertje and return to Steenstraat. Go back across Simon Stevin Plein and Oud Burg and bear to the left. Instead of going back down Mariastrat, take the street to the left, which is Nieustraat. You'll cross a bridge and be on Dijver. Turn left and on the right you will find Den Dyver.

Den Dyver on Dijver

Dijver 5
Phone: 32 50 33 60 69
www.dijver.be

This restaurant is one of the best in Bruges and not just because of its beer connection, although for beer lovers, that helps. Den Dyver is a family-owned business that has chosen to build its menu around pairing delicious gourmet foods with the appropriate beer selection—much like wine sommeliers might do.

The concept may strike some as odd at first but it's amazing how the food and the beers enhance one another. This is not a place for a quick drink, but a place to enjoy the food and the beers. Reservations are recommended because this can be a popular place to linger for lunch or dinner.

When you exit Den Dyver, turn right and cross the street. At the next bridge, turn left on Wollestraat. There is a small courtyard on your right through arches. The Erasmus restaurant is located in the Hotel Erasmus, which will be on your left after you enter the courtyard.

Erasmus

Wollestraat 35
Phone: 32 50 33 57 81
www.hotelerasmus.com/index.html
The little boutique hotel has an exceptional brasserie that features wines as well as beers, but beer is what people come to Erasmus for. There are no bottles here, just beers brewed and served in small barrels. Tastings are almost essential. The proprietors pride themselves with only serving what they consider to be the results of the artisanship of small Flemish family breweries. The kitchen serves small dishes and pastas that are perfect for the accompanying brews served. The 8-10 draught beers change monthly.

Cross the courtyard to the 2BE shop.

2BE

Wollestraat 53
Phone: 32 50 611 222
www.2-be.biz
By now, I'm sure you are anxious to take some of these beers home. 2BE is a great place to start stocking up. The wall of 780 beer bottles outside should give a hint of what's available inside. The 2BE shop was opened in 2006 and offers only Belgian-made products. That means a lot of beer. There are more than 400 beers available for you to purchase.

When you exit 2BE, turn left on Wollestraat, away from the canal. Just before you get to the Markt, there is a pedestrian street to the right next to the Post Office. Turn right on Breidelstraat. After a hundred metres or more you will see a small alley labelled De Garre in between a line of shops. Turn right.

De Garre

De Garre 1
Phone: 32 50 34 10 29

De Garre is another one of those places in Bruges that are considered a rite of passage to those in search of the best beers. This tiny, old, two-storey building is generally full of as many locals as it is tourists so you almost have to gauge your arrival time to get a seat.

The rooms are small, the bar is small, but the beer is big. 11% to be exact. The house beer is Triple de Garre and after a taste, you'll understand why this place is so popular. Of course, if you opt to try something else, there are hundreds to choose from.

Exit De Garre and go back towards the Markt. Turn right and go straight along the government buildings and up the street directly across the square. This is Vlamingstraat. Taverna Curiosa is on the right a few streets in.

Taverna Curiosa

Vlamingstraat 22
Phone: 32 50 34 23 34
www.curiosa-brugge.com

Venture down the stairs to this medieval cellar turned cosy restaurant and you'll be tempted to stay. Taverna Curiosa was exactly that—a tavern—when it was founded in the late 1980s. And although it is still a place to come and enjoy beers, it now prides itself in offering a menu of succulent meat dishes or fresh fish prepared in a variety of ways.

Exit Curiosa and turn right on Philipstockstraat.

Cambrinus

....

Philipstockstraat 19
Phone: 32 50 33 23 28
www.cambrinus.eu

This restaurant calls itself a "bierbrasseie" and is named after the legendary king of beers, Cambrinus, who was credited with inventing beer itself. Its vast beer menu even carries offerings of up to 13% alcohol content.

Beers are the central focal point of the restaurant, which is also has a significant menu. They even offer something called the "Menu of the Brewers", which includes Trappists' cheese croquettes, Flemish carbonades in "Gulden Draak" beer sauce and a crème brûlée with Dark Abbey beer.

It's obvious from the building's façade that it has always had a soft spot for beer. The building was built in 1699 and on one corner of the exterior you will find a statue sitting on a large vat, holding a foaming mug of beer in his hand.

Also depicted are Venus, Roman goddess of love, representing spring; Ceres, goddess of agriculture, representing summer; Bacchus, god of wine, representing autumn; and Diana, goddess of the hunt and the moon, representing winter. You will also find the Devil, the Sun and the Moon on the exterior.

Go back to Vlamingstraat and turn right. De Zolder Keldercafe will be only a few streets up, just past Academiestrasse.

De Zolder Keldercafe

....

Vlamingstraat 53
Phone: 32 4 77 24 49 05
www.keldercafedezolder.be

The name defies the location for De Zolder Keldercafe. Translated, it means "attic". But this is another pub located in a cellar. In fact, a sign above the door boasts that it is "Bruges' Cosiest Cellar". The selection is not as vast here, but it is still noteworthy, specializing in barrel beers. The beer menu is varied and changes. There is typically a younger crowd here, who are drawn to the good prices.

Exit De Zolder Keldercafe and double back to Academiestrasse and turn left. Bacchus Cornelius is just half a street in.

Bacchus Cornelius

Academiestraat 17
Phone: 32 50 34 53 38
www.bacchuscornelius.com

If you want to start purchasing beer to take home, this is the place. It's easy to see why Bacchus Cornelius is touted as the best bottle shop in Bruges. Pricing is reasonable and they offer more than 450 different beers.

The beers are arranged by style and you'll be amazed at the variety. The staff are extremely helpful and knowledgeable. If they are out of something you want, they can easily suggest something comparable.

Bacchus also sells glasses and memorabilia as well as a local concoction called jenevers (often called Holland Gin). You many even get a sample!

Exit Bacchus Cornelius and continue down Academiestraat. When you get to the canal and the statue of Jan Van Eyck, bear to your right and go along the right side of the canal on Spinolarei. Follow the canal until it intersects another canal and cross over that bridge. Continue across the street St Annarei and head down the street in front of you called Blekersstraat. Café Vlissinghe will be a street in on your right.

Café Vlissinghe

Blekersstraat 2
Phone: 32 50 34 37 37
www.cafevlissinghe.be

The perfect place to end your beer walk. Continuously in operation for almost 500 years, Café Vlissinghe is worth the extra effort it takes to find it. This is not just Bruges' oldest pub. It's one of the oldest pubs in the entire world, showing up on maps dating back to the 17th century. Tucked down a narrow street in Bruges' quiet St Anna District, this quaint establishment was once "the bar" for merchants and seamen during the city's heyday as a port.

As you enter the foyer of the building, there is a list of all the owners dating back to the beginning. Little has changed over the centuries. The biggest difference is that the café used to be located on what was virtually beachfront property. Now, the coast is 56 km (35 mi) away. In fact, the name itself means "wet soil" or "beach". The décor looks the same and it is even still heated by an old stove. You could close your eyes and almost imagine the sailors who passed their time drinking here.

There are three beers on tap and about 24 others to choose from. Café Vlissinghe also serves good snacks, salads and starters. Still, you can't beat the ambience. There are the locals who frequent the place and they more often than not outnumber the tourists. During the summer, there is a fabulous beer garden out the back.

Centuries of beer drinking can affirm your urge to kick back and just stay here and enjoy history while drinking beer.

Things You Should
Know About

It's not just about walking, is it? There is dining, sleeping and taking in of the culture, which must be enjoyed as well.

The following chapters will give you some guidance to places you will likely experience on or near one of the walks, as well as some general information that could be useful during your stay.

Helpful Information

This section includes all of those important titbits of information that you may find yourself searching for.

ATMs

- **Brugge-Hoofdhuis**
  S.A. Generale De Banque
  Vlamingstraat 38-39
- **Fortis Bank**
  Simon Stevinplein 3
- **Citibank, N.A.**
  Noordzandstraat 57
- **Fortis Bank**
  Vlamingstraat 78
- **De Post**
  Markt 5
- **Ing Belgique S.A.**
  Markt 18-19
- **Europabank**
  Vlamingstraat 13
- **KBC**
  Steenstraat 38-40
- **Fortis Bank**
  Noordzandstraat 95

Banks

Most banks are open Monday-Friday, 9am-3.30pm or 4pm and closed on Saturdays, Sundays and holidays. Some banks are open until 11am on Saturday or could be closed during lunch hours during the week.

Bureaus de Change

Most banks will exchange money, but exchange services are available at this location:

- **Goffin Change**
  Steenstraat 2

- **Pillen R.W.J.**
  Rozenhoedkaai 2

Bruges Card

Although it is issued through a private entity, the Bruges Card works with many tourism operations and can help you obtain discounts on shopping, museums, bike rental, bars and restaurants.

The card is free and can be picked up at many hotels and hostels, or contact:
- **Bruges Card**
  pa. Travel-Europe bvba
  Langestraat 145
  B-8000 Bruges, Belgium
  info@brugescard.be

Carillon Concerts

Concerts on the Belfry Carillon are:

October-Mid June: Sunday, Wednesday, Saturday 2.15-3pm
Summer Season: Monday, Wednesday, Saturday 9am-10pm,
                    Sunday 2.15-3pm
New Year's Day: 2pm

Consulates in Bruges

- **Croatian Consulate**
  Diksmuidse Heerweg 126
  8200 Bruges
  Phone: 32 50 39 35 55

- **Honorary French Consulate**
  Bruges
  Phone: 32 50 35 05 33
  Email: *r.zonnekein@pi.be*

- **Royal Danish Consulate**
  Gemene Weideweg Noord 34
  8310 Bruges
  Phone: 32 50 35 63 64
  Hours: 8am-12pm, 1pm-5pm

Embassies in Belgium

There are more than 200 embassies of foreign lands located in Belgium, most of which are located in Brussels, just an hour away from Bruges. Below is a list of some key embassies and their contact information.

- **Argentina Embassy**
  Avenue Louise 225, 3rd floor, 1050 Brussels
  Phone: 32 26 47 78 12
  Hours: 32 26 47 78 12
  Email: info@embargentina.be

- **Irish Embassy**
  Rue Wiertz 50, 1050 Brussels
  Phone: 32 22 35 66 76
  Email: embirl@online.be

- **Australian Embassy**
  Rue Guimardstraat 6-8, 1040 Brussels
  Phone: 32 22 86 05 00
  Hours: Monday-Friday 8.30am-5pm, except for public holidays
  Email: PubAffs.Brussels@dfat.gov.au
  Website: www.austemb.be

- **Israeli Embassy**
  Av. de l'Observatoire 40, 1180 Brussels
  Phone: 32 23 73 55 00
  Hours: 9.30am-12.30pm
  Email: brussels@israel.org
  Website: www.brussels.mfa.gov.il

- **Brazilian Embassy**
  Av. Louise 350, Boîte 5 (6ème étage), 1050 Brussels

Phone: 32 26 40 20 15
Email: brasbruxelas@beon.be

- **Embassy of Japan**
  Avenue des Arts/Kunstlaan 58, 6th Floor, 1000 Brussels
  Telephone: 32 25 13 23 40
  Hours: Monday-Friday, 9.30am-12pm & 1.30-4pm
  Website: www.be.emb-japan.go.jp

- **Embassy of Britain**
  Rue d'Arlon 85, Brussels
  Phone: 32 22 87 62 11
  Hours: Monday-Friday:
  Embassy: 0900-1730
  Consular: 9am-12.30pm & 2.15-4pm
  Visa: 9-11.30am
  Email: info@britain.be
  consularsection.Brussels@fco.gov.uk
  Website: www.britishembassy.gov.uk/belgium

- **Norwegian Embassy**
  Rue Archimède 17, 1000 Brussels
  Phone: 32 26 46 07 80
  Email: em.brussels@mfa.no
  Website: www.norvege.be

- **Embassy of Canada**
  Avenue de Tervueren 2, 1040 Brussels
  Phone: 32 27 41 06 11
  Hours: Monday-Friday: 9.00am-12.30pm & 1.30-5pm
  Email: bru@dfait-maeci.gc.ca
  bru@international.gc.ca
  Website: www.ambassade-canada.be

- **Embassy of Pakistan**
  57 Avenue Delleur, 1170 Brussels
  Phone: 32 2 673 80 07
  Hours: 9am-12pm
  Email: parepbrussels@skynet.be

Website: www.embassyofpakistan.be

- **Chilean Embassy**
  Rue des Aduatiques 106, 1040 Brussels
  Phone: 32 27 43 36 60
  Email: embachile@embachlle.be
  Website: www.embachile.be
  Hours: 9am-4pm

- **Embassy of the Philippines**
  297 Avenue Moliere, 1050 Brussels
  Phone: 32 23 40 33 77

- **China Embassy**
  400 Boulevard du Souverain, 1160 Auderghem, Brussels
  Phone: 32 27 79 43 33
  Email: chinaemb be@mfa.gov.cn
  Website: www.chinaembassy-org.be

- **Embassy of the Russian Federation**
  Avenue de Fre, 66, 1180 Brussels
  Phone: 32 23 74 34 00
  Email: ambrusbel@skynet.be
  Website: www.belgium.mid.ru

- **Egyptian Embassy**
  Av. de l'Uruguay 19, 1000 Brussels
  Phone: 32 26 63 58 00/20/28
  Email: embassy.egypt@skynet.be

- **Saudi Arabian Embassy**
  Avenue Franklin Roosevelt, 45, 1050 Brussels
  Phone: 32 26 49 20 44
  Hours: 9am-3pm
  Email: beemb@mofa.gov.sa

- **Embassy of Fiji**
  Square Plasky, 92–94, 1030 Brussels
  Phone: 32 27 36 90 50

Hours: Monday-Friday 9am–1pm & 2pm- 5pm

- **Singapore Embassy**
  98 Avenue Franklin Roosevelt, 1050 Brussels
  Phone: 32 26 60 29 79
  Hours: Monday-Friday 8.30am-12.30pm & 1.30-5pm
  Email: amb.eu@singembbru.be
  Website: www.mfa.gov.sg/brussels

- **Embassy of Finland**
  Avenue des Arts 58, B-1000 Brussels
  Phone: 32 22 87 12 12
  Hours: 9am-1pm
  Email: sanomat.bry@formin.fi
  Website: www.finlande.be

- **South African Embassy**
  Rue Montoyer 17-19, 1000 Brussels
  Phone: 32 22 85 44 00
  Hours: Monday-Thursday 8.30am–5pm,
  Friday 8.30am–3.45pm
  Email: embassy@southafrica.be
  Website: www.southafrica.be

- **French Embassy**
  65 rue Ducale, 1000 Brussels
  Phone: 32 25 48 87 11
  Website: www.ambafrance-be.org

- **Embassy of Spain**
  Wetenschapsstraat, 19, 1040 Brussels, Belgium.
  Tel: 32 22 30 03 40
  Email: ambespbe@mail.mae.es

- **German Embassy**
  Tervurenlaan/Avenue de Tervueren 190, 1150 Brüssels
  Phone: 32 27 74 19 11
  Email: info@bruessel.diplo.de
  Website: www.bruessel.diplo.de

- **Royal Embassy of Thailand**
  Square du Val de la Cambre, 2 Brussels
  32 26 40 68 10
  Hours: Monday-Friday 9am-12.30pm & 2–5pm
  Email: thaibxl@thaiembassy.be
  Website: www.thaiembassy.be

- **Embassy of India**
  217 Chaussee De Vleurgat, 1050 Brussels
  Phone: 32 26 40 91 40
           32 26 45 18 50
  Hours: Monday–Friday 9am-5.45pm, 1-1.45pm lunch

- **Embassy of United Arab Emirates**
  73 Av. F. Roosevelt 1050

- **Brussels**
  Phone: 32 26 40 60 00
  Email: uae-embassy@skynet.be
  Website: www.uaeembassybrussels.be

- **Embassy of Indonesia**
  Avenue de Tervueren, 294, Brussels 1150
  Phone: 32 27 71 20 14
  Email: kbribxl@brutele.be
  Website: www.homeusers.brutele.be/kbribxl

- **United States of America Embassy**
  Regentlaan 27, Boulevard du Regent, B 10000 Brussels
  Phone: 32 25 08 21 11
  Hours: Monday-Friday 9am-6pm
  Email: www.brussels.usembassy.gov

Service	Phone Number
Police	101
Ambulance & Fire	100
Accidents (this number is valid for all of Europe)	112
Red Cross	105
Child Focus	110
Citizens Advice	106
Burns	0 92 40 34 90
Poisons	0 70 24 52 45
Directory Assistance in Belgium	1207
Directory Assistance - International	1204

Electricity

Throughout Belgium, 220 volts, 50 MHz, is in use. The plug is round.

Internet Cafés

Most hotels have internet connections, but if you are in need while you are out and about, here are the places that offer public access.

- **Bauhaus**
  Langestraat 135, 8000 Bruges
  Phone: 32 50 34 10 93
  Website: www.bauhaus.be

- **Teleboetiek**
  hoek Langestraat-Predikherenstraat, 8000 Bruges
  Phone: 32 50 34 74 72

- **Snuffel Backpackers Hostel**
  Ezelstraat 47, 8000 Bruges
  Phone: 32 50 33 31 33
  Website: www.snuffel.be

Markets

There are numerous markets designed for the locals that should be taken advantage of by visitors. They include:

- **Wednesday**: 7am-1pm on Markt square (food)
- **Saturday**: 8am-1pm on 't Zand square and on Beursplein (food and goods)
- **Sunday**: 8am-1pm on Ten Briele (food and goods)
- **Fish market**, Tuesday-Saturday: every morning on Vismarkt.
- **Flea market**, Saturday & Sunday: 10am-6pm (March 15-November 15) along Dijver and at Fish Market.

Medical

In case of Medical Emergency call 100, but below are numbers and services that you may want to know about.

- **Doctor on duty after hours (**7pm-8am): 32 50 78 15 15 90
- **Pharmacists** (9am–10pm): 32 90 01 05 00
- **Pharmacist** (10pm–9am): 101

Hospital	Phone Number
Academisch Ziekenhuis Sint-Jan Riddershove 10	32 50 45 21 11
AZ Sint- Lucas St Luca Striking 29	32 50 36 91 11
Sint Franciscus Xaveriuskliniek Spaanse Loskaai 1	32 50 47 04 70

National Public Holidays

- New Year's Day - January 1
- Easter - March/April
- Labour Day - May 1
- Ascension Day - 40th day following Easter
- Whit Monday - 7th Monday following Easter
- Luxembourg National Day - June 23

- Festival of the Flemish Community - July 11 (Flanders only)
- National Belgium Day - July 21
- Assumption - August 15
- Walloon Community - September 27
- All Saints' Day - November 1
- Armistice Day - November 11
- Christmas Day - December 25

Post Office

The Main Post Office is located in Markt Square, just next to the Belfry.

Address: Markt 5
Phone: 32 50 33 14 11
Hours: Monday-Friday ,9am-6pm; Saturday, 9am-3pm

Shopping

The main shopping streets are situated between Markt square and the old city gates:

Steenstraat, Simon Stevinplein, Mariastraat, Zuidzandstraat, St-Jakobsstraat, St-Amandsstraat, Geldmuntstraat, Noordzandstraat, Smedenstraat, Vlamingstraat, Philipstockstraat, Academiestraat, Hoogstraat, Langestraat, Smedenstraat, Katelijnestraat, Gentpoortstraat. Between Noordzandstraat and Zuidzandstraat you will find the cosy shopping centre Zilverpand.

- Most shops are open from 9am-6pm (some shops have late night shopping on Friday).
- The main supermarkets are situated just outside the city centre (open 9am-8pm, Fridays till 9pm).

Taxis

As mentioned in Getting There, Getting Around, taxis are plentiful but in general need to be booked. There is a €4,50 minimum charge so if you can walk it, do. Taxi stands are found at the railway station and also in the Markt.

The numbers are:

Markt - 32 50 33 44 44
Stationsplein- 32 50 38 46 50

Tipping
....

Service charges and VAT are always included in the price at a restaurant. However, for exceptional service tip at your discretion. Suggested tip for:
- Portage of luggage: €1 per person.
- Coatroom attendants: €1,25 to €2,50 per coat.
- Toilet attendants: €0.25 to €0.50.

Tourism
....

The official address is:

Bruges Tourism office
PB 744
B-8000 Brugge
Phone : 32 50 44 46 46
Fax : 32 50 44 46 45
toerisme@brugge.be
www.brugge.be
The Office to visit for information is:
In&Uit [Concertgebouw]
't Zand 34
B-8000 BRUGGE
Hours: 10am-6pm. Daily except Christmas Day and New Year's Day.

Museums

There are numerous museums in Bruges to pique a variety of visitors' interests. Some are on the walks. Others are not. But this gives you an insight to what is out there. There are cultural museums, a lace museum, a chocolate museum, a diamond museum and even a museum for French fries or chips!

Sixteen of Bruges' best-known historical sites are also museums. They are part of the Bruggemuseum (Bruges Museum), which groups the museums according to the theme of their location. If you are planning to visit several, it may be a good idea to buy a museum pass for €15, which allows you to visit up to five museums.

Museum	Address	Prices		Opening Hours
		Indi-vidual	Reduc-tions	
Groeninge Museum	Dijver 12	€8	€5	9.30am-5pm
Arents House	Dijver 16	€8	€5	9.30am-5pm
Gruuthuse Museum	Dijver 17	€6	€4	9.30am-5pm
Church of Our Lady	Mariastraat 8	€2,50	€1,50	9.30am-2.30pm 1.30-5pm Saturday closed at 4pm; Sunday closed till 1.30pm
The Archaeological Museum	Mariastraat 36a	€6	€4	9.30am-12.30pm 1.30-5pm
Belfry: Salvador Dalí	Markt 7	€10	€8	10am-6pm
Gothic Chamber of Bruges Town Hall	Burg 12	€2,50	€1,50	9.30am-5pm
Renaissance Hall of the Liberty of Bruges	Burg 11a	€2,50	€1,50	9.30am-12.30pm 1.30-5pm
Memling Museum - St John's Hospital	Mariastraat 38	€8	€5	9.30am-5p
Museum of our Lady of the Potterie	Potterie 79	€8	€5	9.30am-12.30pm 1.30-5pm
St Janshuis Mill	Kruisvest	€2	€1	9.30am-12.30pm 1.30-5pm Open from May 1 until September 30

Koelewei Mill	Kruisvest	€2	€1	9.30am-12.30pm 1.30-5pm Conditionally open from June 1 until September 30
Museum of Folklore	Balstraat 43 & Rolweg 40	€3	€2	9.30am-5pm
Guido Gezelle Museum	Rolweg 64	€2	€1	9.30am-12.30pm 1.30-5pm

Free Entrance for Children under the age of 13

Pass: 5 museums for €15

Reductions: Min. 15 persons, also for senior citizens aged 60 and over

Tickets till 4.30pm, Belfry till 4.15pm

All museums are closed on January 1, Ascension day (afternoon) and December 25

Bruggemuseum Descriptions

The Archaeological Museum
....

Mariastraat 36 A
Hours: Daily except Monday, 9.30am-12.30pm, 1.30-5pm
Entrance Fee: €6, Reduced €4

The Archaeological Museum is an interactive exhibit built around archaeological finds discovered in and around Bruges. The exhibit covers the city's history from the Stone Age to the Middle Ages and includes pottery, glass, leather, metal, wood and stone items, and a series of murals. The daily life of each historical period is tracked through four themes: housing, working, living and dying. Part of the interactive feature puts you to the test to solve an archaeological mystery.

The Belfry
....

Markt 7
Hours: Daily except Monday, 9.30am-5pm (except Easter & Whit Monday)
Entrance Fee: €10, Reduced €8

The Belfry tower is an impressive 83m high and has become the iconic symbol of Bruges. You can climb the 366 steps to the top of the tower for an amazing view of the whole city as well as a close peek at Bruges Carillon, renowned for its 47 bells of various sizes. Along the way, you will also pass the old treasury room.

Your athletic efforts will be rewarded with a breathtaking view of Bruges and its surrounding countryside.

Brangwyn Museum – Arentshuis

Dijver 16
Hours: Daily except Monday, 9.30am-5pm (except Easter & Whit Monday)
Entrance Fee: €8, Reduced €5 (includes Groeninge)
The 18th-century townhouse is now a museum dedicated to the works of Bruges-British artist Frank Brangwyn (1867-1956). He was known for his realistic paintings and watercolours depicting the hard world of the docks and factories of the late 19th and early 20th centuries. Among his many other talents was furniture-making and tapestries. The house is also home to a lace museum.

The Church of Our Lady (Notre Dame) – Onze-Lieve-Vrouwekerk

Mariastraat 8
Hours: Monday-Friday 9.30am-12.30pm, 1.30-5pm; Saturday closed at 4pm; Sunday closed till 1.30pm
Entrance Fee: €2,50, Reduced €1,50
The Church of Our Lady is the tallest building in Bruges. Its 118-m high brick tower has dominated the skyline for centuries. Inside you will find incredible works of art, including a white marble sculpture of the Madonna and Child created by Michelangelo. While much of the church is free to the public, there is a small museum that includes artwork owned by the church. Another big attraction is the tombs of the Dukes of Burgundy, including Mary of Burgundy and her father Charles the Bold.

Folklore Museum

Balstraat 43 and Rolweg 40
Hours: Daily except Monday, 9.30-5pm (except Easter & Whit Monday)
Entrance Fee: €3, Reduced €2
The Folklore Museum is located in a cluster of eight restored 17th-century almshouses that look a great deal like the other almshouses you will see throughout the city. These particular homes belonged to a cobblers' guild. The Folklore Museum has a large number of historic objects depicting days gone by. There are examples of a historic classroom, cobbler's and hatter's workshops, a Flemish living room, an old kitchen, a confectioner's, an old chemist and even an inn called De Zwarte

Kat ("The Black Cat"). If you are there on a Thursday afternoon, you'll see them make fresh sweets from traditional recipes and you can sample them as well.

Genpoort Museum

Geenpoortstraat
Open: Summer months 9.30am-12.30pm, 2.30-5pm, only on request.
This former city gate was originally constructed in 1297. About 150 years later, it was rebuilt along with Kateljnepoort and Kruispoort by Jan van Oudenaarde. In 2008, a museum was opened in the upper floor of the building where a great room runs the full length. Gentpoort features the story of all of the gates as well as the ramparts.

Gothic Chamber of Bruges Town Hall

Burg 12
Hours: Daily except Monday, 9.30am-5pm (except Easter & Whit Monday)
Entrance Fee: €2,50, Reduced €1,50
Decorated with statues of knights, the Town Hall was constructed in 1376 and is one of the oldest gothic city halls in the region. You'll be impressed by what is known simply as "Gothic Hall", which is noteworthy because of its beautiful wooden ceiling and 19th-century wall paintings. Many works of art and documents showing the city's opulent history are exhibited in this room. They are arranged in a manner to tell the story of the Town Council and its relationships with both "higher authorities" and the local people.

Groeninge Museum

Dijver 12
Phone: 32 50 44 87 11
Hours: Daily except Monday, 9.30am-5pm (except Easter & Whit Monday)
Entrance Fee: €8, Reduced €5
Built on the site of a former Eeckhout Abbey, the Groeninge Museum is on the right at the corner of Dijver and Groeninge. It's known as Bruges Museum of Fine Arts, with works dating back to the 16th century. Best known are the Flemish Primitives by Jan van Eyck and Hans Memling. Van Eyck was considered the first and most important "Flemish Primitive" painter and he is honoured throughout Bruges. The museum also contains a unique collection of works by Flemish expressionists as well as a section devoted to Renaissance and Baroque paint

Gruuthuse Museum

Dijver 17
Phone: 32 50 44 87 11
Hours: Daily except Monday, 9.30am-5pm (except Easter & Whit Monday)
Entrance Fee: €6, Reduced €4

This city palace was at one time the residence of the Lords of Gruuthuse. Converted into a museum in 1955, the museum has a far-reaching series of displays that depict life between the 15th and 19th century. Among them: furniture, kitchen equipment, silverware, tapestries, lace, ceramics, glassware, weaponry, music- and measuring-instruments, and more. Its most noteworthy room is called the Room of Honour and contains tapestries, an impressive fire-place and richly decorated timber.

Guido Gezelle Museum

Rolweg 64
Hours: Daily except Monday, 9.30am-12.30pm, 1.30-5pm (except Easter & Whit Monday)
Entrance Fee: €2, Reduced €1

The Guido Gezelle Museum is one of the most important literary museums in all of Flanders. This is the birthplace of the famous 19th-century Flemish poet and contains a host of documents and books connected to the life of the poet-priest. Gezelle was born here in 1830, where his parents were working as caretakers in exchange for room and board.

As a child, he and his friends were notorious mischief makers, terrorizing the neighbourhood. They earned the nickname De Wildewegen van de Rolleweg or "The Rollewey Tearaways". Mario Bloom used the same name for his 1999 comic that pertained to Geselle's political stance. The house and its garden are located in a quiet neighbourhood near the windmills. The garden features the sculpture "The Man Who Gives Fire" by Jan Fabre. Giselle was also a patron of the St Walburgha's Church.

Koelewei Mill

Kruisvest
Hours: Conditionally daily June 1-September 30, 9.30am-12.30pm, 1.30-5pm
Entrance Fee: €2, Reduced €1

The Koelewei Mill has been standing since 1765 and is still going strong in the summer months as an active mill. Along with the Sint-Janshuis Mill, Koelewei (which means "cool meadow") makes up the Bruggemuseum-Molens (or the Mill Museum). The mill was moved from its original location to its current spot near the Dam Gate of Bruges. Visitors are allowed to climb to the top of the millhouse and can see it in operation as long as you visit during the spring and summer months when it is fully functional.

Memling Museum - The Hospital of St John

Mariastraat 38
Hours: Daily except Monday, 9.30am-5pm (except Easter & Whit Monday)
Entrance Fee: €8, Reduced €5
Sint-Janshospitaal is the old city hospital of Bruges and gives a great depiction of what life was life in a medieval hospital ward. Visitors can get a real insight to how the nuns and friars were able to care for the ill throughout the centuries. The hospital chapel contains six paintings by noted Flemish artist Hans Memling. Four of the works were painted specifically for the sisters of the hospital.

Another highlight of the museum is something called the Ursula Shrine, which is a wooden reliquary depicting the life of 4th-Century Breton princess and martyr Ursula. According to legend, the decorated coffer contains not only Ursula's ashes, but those of 11,000 virgins who died with her. Saint John's was used as a hospital from 1188 until 1978. The huge complex also houses a nunnery, a friars' abbey, medieval infirmaries and an old pharmacy.

Our Lady of the Potterie Museum

Potterie 79
Hours: Daily except Monday, 9.30am-12.30pm, 1.30-5pm (except Easter & Whit Monday)
Entrance Fee: €8, Reduced €5
Our Lady of the Potteries is better known for its Baroque church and its outstanding silverwork. The church and its hospital complex were built in the 13th century to service pilgrims and the sick.

The complex is still in use with the elderly now residing in a newer building on the property while the older buildings house the museum. The museum holds an impressive collection of works of art, including objects related to healthcare, worship and the monastery.

Renaissance Hall of the Liberty of Bruges

Burg 11a
Hours: Daily except Monday, 9.30am-12.30pm, 1.30-5pm (except Easter & Whit Monday)
Entrance Fee: €2,50, Reduced €1,50
Liberty of Bruges was built in 1534 and is recognizable because of its somewhat gilded façade. It originally housed the local courts of justice and is now the repository for the Town Archives. The Renaissance Chamber in the interior is noted for a massive fireplace. Made of wood, marble and alabaster, it was built in the 16th century by Lanceloot Blondeel

St John's House Mill (Sint-Janshuysmolen)

Kruisvest
Hours: Daily, May 1–September 30, 9.30am-12.30pm, 1.30-5pm
Entrance Fee: €2, Reduced €1
Bruges once had 29 mills scattered about. Only four now can be found in the city. The Sint-Janshuysmolen was built in 1770 and is the oldest of the mills still standing in its original position. For that matter, it is also the only mill still working regularly. Constructed by a group of 26 bakers, it still functions as an active grain mill as well as a museum. Combined with the Koelewei Mill further up Kruisvest or the embankment that circles Bruges, the two mills make up what is called the Bruggemuseum-Molens (or the Mill Museum).

The rectangular wooden body of the mill is supported by a trestle consisting of the trunks of eight trees. It's designed to rotate around a main post so that the wings will face the wind. Brave souls can also climb a steep, narrow staircase to the top of the main wheelhouse. The mill stands on a mound that dates back to 1297 and it is on the same site where another mill that serviced the St John's Hospital had stood previous. That mill was destroyed by wind in 1744.

Private Museums

Basilica of the Holy Blood

Burg 13
Phone: 32 50 33 67 92
Hours: Daily April-September, 9.30am-12pm, 2-6pm; Daily October-March 10am-12pm, 2-4pm (closed Wednesday afternoon)

www.holyblood.org
Entrance Fee: €1,50, Reduced €1
The church itself gets its name because it purports to house a piece of cloth on which Christ's blood was wiped at His crucifixion. There are two chapels housed in the stone structure tucked in a corner of the Burg. On ground level is the humble St Basil's Chapel (1139-1149) while the upper floor is both the museum and the church where the relic is displayed. The museum displays the reliquary of the Holy Blood, treasures from the chapel, clerical vestments and paintings. The relic, which was brought to Bruges in 1150 by Count of Flanders Diederik van de Elzas, is exhibited daily.

Beguine's House
....

Begijnhof, Wijngaardstraat
Phone: 32 50 44 87 23
Hours: 10am-12pm, 1.45-5pm
Entrance Fee: €2, Reduced €1,50
This historic home is located just inside the gate to the Convent across the bridge from Love Lake. The Beguine's House provides a good picture of the day-to-day life of the women who inhabited this convent from 1245 to 1928. A simple home, it has a few starkly furnished rooms that show their simple lifestyle and includes a small inner garden with a well.

Bladelin Court
....

Hof Bladelin, Naaldenstraat 19
Hours: Monday–Saturday, 9am-12pm, 2-5pm
Entrance Fee: €1
This lovely brick home was built circa 1435 by Pieter Bladelin, treasurer of the Order of the Golden Fleece. The walls surrounding the charming inner garden show impressive stone medallions representing portraits of the former inhabitants. In the 19th century the priest Leon de Foere established a lace school here.

Brewery De Halve Maan
....

Walplein 26
Phone: 32 50 33 26 97
www.halvemaan.be
Hours: April-October, Monday-Friday, 11am-4pm; Saturday 11am-5pm;

Sunday 11am-4pm; November-March, Monday-Friday, 11am-3pm; Saturday-Sunday 11am-4pm
Entrance Fee: €5,50 (includes beer tasting)
Still a very active brewery with a well-visited restaurant and pub, De Halve Moon also functions as a museum, so as long as you've come to sample, you might as well learn about the history of beer and this brewery. A brewery has stood on this site since the 16th century. Henry Maes took over the operations in 1856 and founded Half Moon Brewery, which is still run by his descendents. In a city that once was home to more than 50 breweries, this alone survives. And even though it has outgrown the site, the owners say that some beer will always be brewed here just because of the building's long history.

Tours travel up 220 steps and offer information on the history of Bruges as well as its beers. The trip to the roof provides a fabulous panorama of the city and will whet your appetite for your drinking and walking. You'll wind through various rooms that are no longer in use but have great history behind them. You'll be able to enjoy a beer tasting of their popular Brugse Zot at the conclusion. Zot means "lunatic" so consider that a warning before you have too many!

Choco-Story

Wijnzakstraat 2 (Sint-Jansplein)
Phone: 32 50 61 22 37
Hours: Daily, 10am-5pm
Closed December 24, 25, 31 and January 1
www.choco-story.be
Entrance Fee: €6 adults, €5 students and over 65s, €4 children aged 6-12 years
This fun museum takes you on the journey from chocolate's beginnings in the ancient Mexican world of the Mayas and the Aztecs to its present days in Bruges. Find out how chocolate went from being a drink worthy of the gods to being that decadent indulgence we all enjoy now. If you didn't know about the chocolate-making process before, you'll find yourself fascinated by its evolution. Make sure you stay for the chocolate-making exhibition to get some excellent samples.

Diamond Museum

Katelijnestraat 43
Phone: 32 50 34 20 56
Hours: 10.30am-5.30pm

Daily polishing demonstration, 12.15pm
www.diamondmuseum.be
Entrance Fee: €6, Reduced €5
Museum and Demonstration: €9, Reduced €7,50

This museum is one of only five diamond museums in the entire world and illustrates the extraordinary history of Bruges as Europe's oldest diamond centre. Visitors not only trace how diamonds are mined and their history, but they can also witness actual cutting demonstrations. Prepare to be dazzled by the mining process and by the jewels you can see, including a replica of the crown of Margaret of York.

The Friet Museum

Vlamingstraat 33
Phone: 32 50 34 01 50
www.frietmuseum.be
Hours: Every day, 10am-5pm
Closed December 24, 25, 31, January 1, January 5-16.
Entrance Fee: €6 adults, €5 students and over 65s, €4 children aged
6-12 years, €1 children aged 3-6 years

Don't call them French Fries. The Belgians maintain that it was they and not the French who first started frying up potato strips so it's fitting that they have the only friet (chips) museum in the world. The museum traces the story of the humble potato from South America and sees how it has evolved into a chip. There is even a Belgian Union of Potato Fryers and the Friet Museum has won several of its awards.

Once your appetite is whetted feel free to try the tasty chips cooked by the man who cooked chips for the Belgian Royal Family. Collector Eddy Van Belle created the Friet Museum in tribute to all things fries. Van Belle also owns the Choco-Story and Lamp Museums.

Lace Centre and Jerusalem Church

Peperstraat 3
Hours: Monday-Friday, 10am-12pm, 2-6pm; Saturday till 5pm
Closed December 25, January 1, Sundays and public holidays
www.kantcentrum.com
Entrance Fee: €2,50, Reduced €1,50, children under 7 free

Lace in Bruges can be traced to 1717 when the Sisters Apostoline set up a lace school in Ganzestraat. The non-profit Kantcentrum was founded in 1970 to make sure this form of art would continue. A large room at the back of the centre usually has several practitioners doing demonstrations and you'll be amazed to see the skill as they weave their spindles of thread around patterns outlined in pins on pillows. A shop in the complex sells church souvenirs as well as lace-making materials. The museum section shows various styles of lace dating back centuries. The Lace Centre shares a complex with a 15th-century church that was built according to the plans of the Holy Sepulchre in Jerusalem. The church itself is also well worth a visit and includes the precious stained glass windows and the mausoleums of the church founders (Anselmus Adornes and his spouse). Located in a quiet area of the city, the church is easily recognizable because of its octagonal tower. The church is still privately owned by descendents of the Adornes.

The Lamp Museum (Lumina Domestica)

Wijnzakstraat 2
Phone: 32 50 61 22 37
Hours: Daily, 10am-5pm
www.luminadomestica.be
Entrance Fee: €10 adults, €8 students and over 65s, €6 children aged
6-12 years
This Museum of Lighting is the largest museum of lighting in the world. Tracing civilization's 400,000 years of struggle against darkness, the museum contains 6,500 lamps. The story starts with the torch and the oil lamp and evolves to the electric bulb and the LED.

St George's Archers Guild (Sint-Joris Gilde)

Stijn Streuvelsstraat 59
Phone: 32 50 33 54 08
Hours: Daily on request
Entrance Fee: €2
This small, but important museum contains a collection of crossbows and paintings as well as the guild's valuable archives.

St Saviour's Cathedral

St.Salvatorkoorstraat 8
Hours: Cathedral: Monday, 2-5.30pm; Tuesday-Friday, 9am–12pm,
2-5.30pm; Saturday, 9am-12pm, 2-3.30pm; Sunday, 9-10am, 2-5pm

Treasury: Sunday–Friday, 2-5pm
www.sintsalvator.be
Entrance Fee: €2,50, Reduced €1,50
St Saviour's is Bruges' oldest parish church (12th-15th century). In addition to the church you will find the Cathedral's treasury. Inside, there are paintings by, among others, Dirk Bouts and Hugo van der Goes. It also holds manuscripts, copper memorial plaques and silver and gold artefacts.

St Sebastian Archers' Guild (Sint-Sebastiaangilde)

Carmersstraat 174
Phone: 32 50 33 16 26
Hours: Summer: Tuesday, Wednesday, Thursday, 10am-12pm; Saturday, 2-5pm; Winter: Tuesday, Wednesday, Thursday, Saturday, 2-5pm
www.sebastiaansgilde.be
The Saint Sebastian Archers' Guild dates back to the Middle Ages, when the group was part of the local militia. The highly respected guild used their skills with the long bow during the crusades and in return were allowed to use the Jerusalem crucifix in their coat of arms. The guild moved into this complex in 1573 and it has seen its share of illustrious guests. The exiled English King Charles II and his brother Henry Stuart, Duke of Gloucester lived here between 1656-1659 and became members of the guild. Paintings of the royal patrons adorn the walls of the royal hall. A vaulted gallery contains a treasure trove of paintings and archives chronicling the guild's rich history. Each floor has a different shape, ranging from round to square to octagonal. In addition to the gallery, the building contains an orchestra room and theatre.

Churches

B y now you will have noticed that there is an incredible number of churches in Bruges and every one is as unique as the city itself. This chapter looks at each and what they are known for architecturally as well as historically. Most still hold services and when possible service hours are listed.

Basilica of the Holy Blood

Burg 13
Phone: 32 50 33 67 92
Worship: Sundays & holidays, 8 am & 11 am
www.holyblood.org
Events: The colourful Procession of the Holy Blood is held on Ascension Day in the spring.
This is one of Bruges' best-known churches and a visit has been a pilgrimage to many. There are two chapels here. On ground level is the humble St Basil's Chapel (1139-1149) while the decorated chapel in the upper floor purports to house a piece of cloth on which Christ's blood was wiped at His crucifixion. The relic, which was brought to Bruges in 1150 by Count of Flanders Diederik van de Elzas, is exhibited daily. The museum displays the reliquary of the Holy Blood, clerical vestments and paintings.

Beguinage Church

Beguinage or Monastery de Wijngaard
Phone: 32 50 33 00 11
Worship: Sunday, 9.30am
The Beguinage Church lies in the centre of the quiet courtyard of the Beguinage. The church was built in 1609 after the original was destroyed in a fire. It was renovated later to its present Baroque style. The church is dedicated to Saint Elizabeth and a painting of her is just one of the many works by J. Van Oost that adorn the church. It was the spiritual centre for the strict beguine religious order until they abandoned the convent in 1928. The church and the Beguinage complex has been the home to Benedictine nuns since 1937.

Capucin Church

Boeveriestraat 18,
Worship: Saturday, 6pm; Sunday, 7am & 10.30am
This convent in a quiet neighbourhood near Bruges' train station was built in 1867-1871 after the monastery on 't Zand was demolished to make way for the construction of the depot. It's a simple, brick church with a small shrine near the entry. The Neo-Baroque-style furniture was made by sculptor Henry Brugse Pickery.

Carmelite's Church

Ezelstraat 28
Phone: 32 50 33 10 50
www.karmelieten.be
Worship: Saturday, 6pm, evening song; Sunday 10am, Gregorian Mass
The Carmelites first came to this location in 1633 to bring their religious teachings to Bruges. The Baroque church was then built in 1688. The nuns were known for their works during the plague and a 17th-century plague house remains in the garden. These days, the complex is always alive with activity. The Gregorian Mass each Sunday is something unique if you have never had the chance to experience it before. In addition, it's known to play host to religious musical performances, so be sure to check their calendar. The church also contains a massive library of religious writings.

Chapel of Our Lady of the Blind

Kreupelenstraat
Events: Procession on August 15. Each year a procession is lead from here to the Potterierrei in honour of the Battle of Pevelenberg in 1304 against the French.
This church was built after a promise made during the battle of Pevelenberg, which claimed numerous lives. As the name suggests, this church was built to service the blind, who were looked after at the adjacent Almshouse. The chapel is located on Cripple Street, which speaks to the mentality of that age where people with disabilities were separated from the rest of the population. Erected in the 14th century, it is surprisingly known for its beautiful interior, including a magnificent pulpit that was built in 1659. The chapel also contains a beautiful, polychrome, gilded statue from the 14th century of Our Lady of the Blind. Take time to enjoy the small garden located next to the church.

English Convent (Engels Klooster)

Carmersstraat 85
Phone: 32 50 33 24 24
www.the-english-convent.be
Worship: Saturday 2.30pm; Sunday 4pm
The nuns at this church are very active and in addition to the regular services, they have rooms available for overnight guests for meditation, meetings, conferences, courses, study or silent days. The convent has been here since 1629 but the richly decorated church was built between 1736 and 1739. Most notable in the one aisle sanctuary is the main altar, which is made of 23 different marble pieces. The convent was founded as a haven for English nuns and monks who were escaping persecution in Britain when King Henry VIII banned Catholicism. It was expanded in the 18th century at which time the domed church was constructed, but the community had to flee when French rule began in 1794. The convent was sold, but the nuns were able to purchase it back in 1804 and turn it into a school. Poet and priest Guideo Geselle took over running the Monastery for a time and eventually died here. The school closed in recent years.

Former Carthusian Nuns Church

Kartuizerinnenstraat
The Carthusian Order was founded in 1084 and this church dates back to 1716. These days, the sanctuary of the complex is used as a military chapel. It's located next to Hotel Orangerie, which is the site of the former convent and overlooks the Dijver Canal.

The Church of Our Lady (Notre Dame) – Onze-Lieve-Vrouwekerk

Mariastraat 8
www.museabrugge.be
Worship: Saturday, 5.30pm; Sunday, 11am
The Church of Our Lady is the tallest building in Bruges. Its 118-m-high brick tower has dominated the skyline for centuries. The church itself dates from the 13th century. Inside you will find incredible works of art, including a white marble sculpture of the Madonna and Child created by Michelangelo. While much of the church is free to the public, there is a small museum that includes artwork owned by the church. Among the other items of interest are the tombs of the Dukes of Burgundy, including Mary of Burgundy and her father Charles the Bold.

Holy Magdalena

Astrid Park
Phone: 32 50 33 68 18
Worship: Sunday, 9.30am
Built in 1853, this is one of Bruges' newer churches. Holy Magdalena was built when the city established Astrid Park. This lovely park was the site of the gardens of a former Franciscan Monastery, which was dissolved in 1796.

Jerusalem Church

Peperstraat 3
Phone: 32 50 33 00 72
The 15th-century Jerusalem Church is rare in that it has been preserved largely in its original state. Built according to the plans of the Holy Sepulchre in Jerusalem, the mausoleums of benefactors Anselmus Adorno and his wife Margaretha vander Banck are located at the centre of the church. The Church is privately owned by the descendants of the Adorno family, who were originally merchants from Genoa. Located in a quiet neighbourhood of the city, this highly unusual church with octagonal tower is set apart from its surroundings. Within the complex is the non-profit Kantcentrum or Lace Centre.

Our Lady of the Potterie Museum and Church

Potterieri 79
Phone: 32 50 44 87 77
www.museabrugge.be
The Baroque Our Lady of the Potterie Museum and its hospital complex were built in the 13th century to service pilgrims and the sick. The older buildings now house a museum while a residential facility for the elderly occupies the newer buildings. The museum that holds Our Lady of the Potterie has existed since the 13th century. Here you'll find an impressive collection of works of art, including objects related to healthcare, worship and the monastery. The museum is part of the Bruggemusea.

Church of St Anne's

St-Annaplein
Worship: Sunday, 10am; closed autumn & winter, open April 1
Events: Easter service
The simple exterior of this church hides an impressive Baroque interior making this church one of Bruges' most impressive. The most noteworthy feature is its

marble rood loft created in 1626 by H. van Mildert. The present Church of St Anne's was consecrated in 1624. It took the place of a former gothic church razed to the ground in 1581. The luxurious interior includes a marble rood screen, choir and confessional stalls known for the unity of their style. The acclaimed Bruges poet Guido Gazelle was baptized in St Anne's.

St Giles

Gillisker
Worship: Sunday, 10am; closed autumn & winter, open April 1
Events: Easter service
St Giles sits in the centre of a square and the neighbourhood grew up around it and is called St Giles Village. The steeple is the only one in Bruges with a clock in it. The church was originally founded in 1240, but the majority of the work was done in the 15th century. The organ is considered one of the best in the city and there are also a number of significant paintings inside, including four by Brugean painter Jan Garemijn depicting the history of the "Trinitarian" brotherhood. Hans Memling, Pierter Pourbus and Lanceloot Blondeel are among those believed to be buried in the churchyard.

St Godelieve's Abbey

Boeveriestraat 45
Phone: 32 50 33 28 98
Worship: Sunday, 7am, 9.30am, 11.45am, 5.15pm, 5.45pm, 8.15pm
The Benedictine abbey was built in 1623 and the monks play an integral role in the surrounding community. St Godelieve's takes up an entire block and there is a constant hub of quiet religious activity. Services are held daily. There is a reflection centre that can house up to 16 guests and includes a chapel and several meeting rooms.

St James' Church (Sint-Jakobskerk)

Ezelstraat and Boterhuis (Sint-Jakobsplein)
Worship: Saturday, 4.30pm
Located in what was the wealthy neighbourhood of Bruges in the 15th century, Sint-Jakobskerk (St James's Church) benefited from those who came here to worship. The Gothic church was founded as a branch of St Saviour's Church in about 1420 during a time of expansion in the city. It was initially built through funds

donated by the Duke of Burgundy, but as the neighbourhood grew, the church became more ornate and known for its art collection. It has several chapels and over 80 paintings inside, including a celebrated depiction of the Legend of St Lucy and a few important works by Pieter Pourbus. St James' oak pulpit is particularly noteworthy for its detailed carvings. It's supported by four figures that represent the known continents of that period: Asia, Africa, America and Europe. Also, notice the Chapel of Ferry de Gros, which contains the mausoleum of Ferry de Gros who was treasurer of the Order of the Golden Fleece. (The Order was an order of knights founded in 1430 by Duke Philip the Good of Flanders.)

St Peter's Chapel,

Keersstraat 1
Worship: Sunday, 10am
Located only a few streets off the Markt, this small church is the former chapel of the candle-makers, today shared by the United Protestant Church and the English Church.

St Saviour's Cathedral (Sint-Salvatorskathedraal)

St.Salvatorkoorstraat 8
Phone: 32 50 86 61 88
www.sintsalvator.be
Worship: April-September, Monday-Friday, 10-11.30am, 2.30-5pm;
Saturday, 10-11.30am, 2.30-4pm; October-March, Monday-Friday, 10-
11.30am, 2.30-4.30pm; Saturday, 10-11.30am, 2.30-4pm
St Saviour's Cathedral is the city's oldest parish church. Originally begun in the 9th century, the vast amount of construction on this building took place between the 12th and 15th centuries. It was originally known simply as St Saviour's Church but was given the designation of Cathedral after Sint-Donatius Cathedral was destroyed by the French in the 19th century.

The high altar was designed by J. Crocx and dates back to 1642. Above it, you will see the three patron saints of the church, Saint Saviour, Saint Donatius and Saint Eligius. In addition to the church, you will find the Cathedral's treasury. Inside, there are paintings by, among others, Dirk Bouts and Hugo van der Goes. It also holds manuscripts and copper memorial plaques, as well as silver and gold artefacts.

St Walburgha's Church (Sint-Walburgakerk)

Koningstraat (Sint-Maartensplein)
Worship: Sunday, 7pm

The Baroque St Walburgha's Church was built in about 1619 by the Jesuit Pieter Huyssensof. It was built as a replica of the Gesù Church in Rome. St Walburgha's was originally attached to a convent and dedicated to St Francis Xavier, whose statue is in a niche above the entrance. It was the main Jesuit church of Bruges until 1774. Deconsecrated in the French Revolution, the Saint-Walburgaparish took over running the church. It was rededicated in 1802. Poet Guido Gezelle was curator for a time before moving to the English Monastery. St Walburgha's contains a marble communion bench, pulpit by Artus Quellin the Younger, high altar and pulpit. In the summer, the church is open to the public every evening.

Speciality Shops

O ne could argue that just about any shop in Bruges is unique, but here are a few offerings that are truly apart from the rest in this special city.

't Apostolientje

Balstraat 11
Phone: 32 50 33 78 60
Open: Daily
While a good deal of the lace you see in shops in Bruges is made by machine, you have assurance that all of the lace sold at 't Apostolientje is handmade. Some of their pieces are antique and incredibly delicate. The shop also sells lace-making materials and can give you excellent information regarding the history of lace and the various qualities of lace.

Atelier Galerie Kasper

Wijngaardstraat 22
Phone: 32 50 34 37 92
www.keremiekkarper.be
Open: Daily
Atelier Galerie Kasper is a great place for unique souvenirs of Bruges. Located very near the Beguinage, everything in this shop is handmade by the artist who also runs the shop. It's fun to just stroll and see the distinctive and often humorous figures, as well as beautiful tiles. Truly every piece is one of a kind.

Antiquariaat Van de Wiele

Sint-Salvatorkerkhof 7
Phone: 32 50 33 63 17
Open: Monday, Thursday 2-6pm; Friday, Saturday 10am-12pm, 2.30-6pm. Closed Tuesday, Wednesday, Sunday
www.marcvandewiele.com
Buying and selling antique books and art in Bruges for more than 30 years, Marc Van de Wiele is an expert antiquarian. Specializing in illustrated books from the 15th-20th century Mr. van de Wiele has a broad and unique selection from which to choose—or to just explore and enjoy. He also conducts several auctions each year.

Au Bonheur des Dames

....

Burgstraat 4
Phone: 32 50 33 39 41
Open: Monday-Saturday, 10.30am-4pm
The name means "The Ladies' Delight". Sophie Verlinde sells collections of buttons, lavender cushions, fine brocade and handmade jewellery.

Bazar Bizar

....

Sint Jakobstraat 305
Phone: 32 50 33 80 16
Open: Daily, 10.30am-6pm; closed Sunday
www.bazarbizar.be
This unique shop offers a wide variety of decorative pieces for those looking for an individual souvenir. The colourful shop carries a wide variety of items ranging from vibrant cushions to candle holders, scarves and even mosquito nets!

Boekhandel De Reyghere

....

Markt 12
Phone: 32 50 49 12 29
Open: Daily, except Sunday
www.dereyghere.be
Located right on the Markt, this book shop has been in operation since 1888. First specializing in newspapers, magazines and English language books, it has grown considerably. Still owned by the original family, it's also a great place to find postcards and small souvenirs as well as books and newspapers in numerous languages. A separate travel selection is found next door.

Bruges Boekhandel

....

Dijver 2
Phone: 32 50 34 68 70
Open: Daily, except Sunday
www.brugesboekhandel.be
Conveniently located on the Dijver Canal near the Fish Market, this book shop is crammed with interesting titles including many foreign books. The helpful staff will assist in locating whatever you may require. The store also includes a good selec-

tion of maps and travel books.

The Chocolate Line

Simon Stevinplein 19
Phone: 32 50 34 10 90
www.thechocolateline.be
In a city filled with chocolate shops, this shop is known for its creativity. Owners Fabienne Destaercke and Dominique Persoone fancy themselves "Shock-o-latiers", combining chocolate with peas, tequila, cola, oysters, chicken—you name it. Even the displays will have you taking photographs if you aren't brave enough to sample. Step outside the box and try one of their unique offerings. It doesn't have to be extreme. Chocolate and garlic perhaps? Or perhaps the chilli-lime?

Danneels

Sint Amandstraat 46
Phone: 32 50 33 31 41
For intrepid travellers, Danneels offers just about every type of luggage or travel accessory you may need. Beautiful leather items of high quality with unique pieces are to be found here.

Delicatessen de Westhoek

Noordsandstraat 39
Phone: 32 50 33 60 32
Open: Daily, except Sunday
Delicatessen de Westhoek has a mouthwatering array of hams, cheeses and sausages as well as homemade dishes, cakes and sweets. Sandwiches are also available. Very much a local favourite, the shop has unique food offerings for you to sample.

Diksmuids Boterhuis

Geldmuntstraat 23
Phone: 32 50 33 32 43
Considered one of the oldest produce shops in Bruges, Diksmuids Boterhuise is a fabulous delicatessen. It has over 300 types of cheese, including 30 regional goat's cheeses.

De Grande Antiques

Vlamingveld 8
Phone: 32 50 81 36 88
www.pauldegrande.com

This antique store boasts the biggest and most original stock of antiques in all of Flanders. In business for almost four decades, they sell items from the 16th century onwards. The pieces are constantly changing, with antiques arriving each week. They will happily arrange shipping for anything you are unable to take with you.

Handwerkhuisje (Eurocrafts)

Katelijnestraat 23
Phone: 32 34 43 50
Open daily 10am- 6pm
www.eurocrafts.com

For more than two decades this shop has specialized in handmade needlework products and the materials with which to make them. They have a great selection of bell pulls and hardware, high quality bobbin lace, beautiful handicraft kits, finely crafted embroidery scissors, and books as well as a wide choice of fabric.

Irma

Oude Burg 4
Phone: 32 50 34 03 33
Open: Daily, 10am-6pm

This wonderful lace shop also holds lace-making demonstrations from 2-6pm each day. It carries a wide selection of intricately handmade lace as well as antique offerings.

Kantjuweeltje

Philipstockstraat 11
Phone: 32 50 33 42 25
Open: Daily, 10am-6pm

The name means "Little Lace Jewel" and is appropriate for this lace shop located in sight of the Belfry. A family tradition since 1895, the shop sells lace and tapestry including cloths, wedding veils, handkerchiefs, blouses and antique lace. There are daily lace-making demonstrations.

Kin Gin

Ezelstraat 227
Phone: 32 50 34 19 09
Open: Daily, except Sunday and Monday
This unique jeweller's studio exhibits its own creations, which are designed and manufactured on site. The pieces include silver and gold, finished with jewels or pearls. They specialize in original and personalized wedding rings.

De Krokodil

Sint-jakobstraat 47
www.krokodil.be
Open: Daily, except Sunday
Even adults become children when they enter this fabulous toy shop. The toys are all designed to be of an educational nature but don't tell the kids that. You won't find electronic games here. Many of the toys are old fashioned, wooden creations that are designed to pique the child's imagination. Krokodil also carries a fine line of children's books, puzzles, board games, technical toys and much more!

Kunst-en Antiekzaak Artifex

Predikherenstraat 2
Phone: 32 50 33 49 22
www.artgalleryartifex.be
This inviting antique shop is known for carrying 19th -20th-century paintings by famous Brugean masters as well as furniture and art objects.

Laurenzino

Noordzandstraat 1
Phone: 32 50 34 58 54
The perfect place to try homemade Belgian waffles. Plain, or topped with caramel or chocolate. If you love ice cream, feel free to indulge.

Milles Fleurs Tapestries

Wollestraat 33
Phone: 32 50 34 54 54

www.millefleurstapestries.com
With some of the finest Belgian tapestries, Mille Fleurs offers a wide selection. An independent company they say they carefully select the best weaving mills in Belgium and other European countries. The shop has been selling wall hangings and tapestry products for more than two decades.

Missault

Braambergstraat 5
Phone: 32 50 33 33 69
Cigar aficionados will enjoy this unique cigar shop, which includes a selection that ranges from Cohiba and Monte Cristo to Romeo y Julieta. It also offers a full range of pipe tobacco.

Musiekhandel Rombaux

Mallebergplaats 13
Open: Monday, 2-6.30pm; Tuesday–Friday, 10am-12.30pm, 2-6.30pm;
Saturday 10am-6pm; closed Sundays
www.rombaux.be
Musiekhandel Rombaux is an amazing music shop that has been around for more than a century. It offers a comprehensive choice of CDs and recordings for everything from classical to jazz. This includes pianos, organs, harps, guitars, strings and sheet music for all instruments.

Oil & Vinegar

Geldmunstraat 11
www.oilvinegar.com
Open: Daily, 10am-6pm; closed Sundays.
This culinary gift shop sells a wide variety of products related to cooking. They feature more than 25 kinds of olive oil, different kinds of vinegar, pesto, bruschetta, spices, pasta, etc. You also can buy several "table necessities" such as special pasta plates, candles and hand-decorated placemats.

The Old Curiosity Shop

Walstraat 8
Phone: 32 50 34 35 91

Open: Daily, 2-6.30pm; closed Mondays.
This fun little shop sells old postcards, stamps, and second hand books. It's a fun place to explore.

La Provence Brugge

Mariastraat 16 & Wijngaardstraat 11
www.laprovence.be
These two locations have wonderful selections of handmade wooden toys.

Theo Wijnhoven

Oostmeers 7
Phone: 32 50 33 36 54
www.theowijnhoven.be
An interior art gallery, Theo Wijnhoven has a unique selection of high-quality pieces. The gallery features a list of prominent international artists. There is no shortage of food and drink in Bruges. Many of the popular restaurants are located around Markt Square but there are hidden gems in the neighbourhoods, some sitting right on the canals. They include the best mussels and the best waffles, traditional dishes from Flanders as well as food from elsewhere in the world. From simple bar meals to some of the finest gourmet dining you will ever experience, Bruges can offer visitors a wide selection from which to choose.

Where to Eat

Au Petit Grand

Philipstockstraat 18
Phone: 32 50 34 86 71
www.aupetitgrand.be
Open: 4pm–12am; closed Monday
Cuisine: Belgian, French, Grill

This quaint restaurant is located near the market and is a favourite among locals. Opened in 2001, it is known for its grilled meats and fish. The staff is attentive and the menu different from most Belgian fare. The house speciality is the Chateaubriand.

Bhavani

Simon Stevinplein 5
Phone: 32 50 33 90 25
www.bhavani.be
Open: Daily, except Wednesday
Cuisine: Indian

Considered some of the best Indian cuisine in Bruges, Bhavani serves a wide range of Indian dishes such as Chicken Tikka Maharaja, Kashmiri Rogan Josh, Tandoori Khazana, Paneer Sagwala and Thali e Bhavani. Decorated with a mixture of colonial charm and exotic Indian colours, this authentic Indian restaurant has a wide selection of foods for both vegetarians and meat eaters.

Bistro de Pompe

Klein St-Amandsstraat 2
Phone: 32 59 61 66 18
www.bistrodepompe.be
Open: 11.30am-10pm; closed Monday
Cuisine: Regional, Belgian

Located in the heart of Bruges near the town pump (hence the name), this restaurant allows you to enjoy fine Belgian cuisine in a casual atmosphere. Also popular with locals, the menu changes according to what is fresh and in season. Good for a quick snack or a three course meal. De Pompe is also open for afternoon tea.

Brasserie Strijdershuis

Hallestraat 14
Phone: 32 50 61 62 60
Open: 10am-12am
Cuisine: Regional, Belgian, French
Located just down a side street from the Belfry, this two-storey bar/restaurant is a good place to grab a beer and a snack or a full blown meal. It opens to a terrace overlooking the street and offers 50 local beers in addition to omelettes and croquets, fish, salads, pasta, pancakes, ice creams and more.

Café Vlissinghe

Blekersstraat 2
Phone: 32 50 34 37 37
www.cafevlissinghe.be
Open: Wednesday-Sunday, 11am–12am
Cuisine: Bar menu
Continuously in operation for almost 500 years, Café Vlissinghe is worth the extra effort it takes to find it. This is Bruges' oldest pub. Tucked down a narrow street in Bruges' St Anna district, it's easy to see why people have been coming to hang out in this bar since the city's early days as a port. The looks have changed little, but it still has some of the best beer in town and is a gathering place for locals as much as out of towners. During the summer, there is a fabulous beer garden at the back. While the real reason to come is the beer, Vlissinghe serves a pretty decent light lunch.

Cafedraal

Zilverstraat 38.
Phone: 32 50 34 08 45
www.cafedraal.be
Open: 12-3pm, 6-11pm; closed Sunday
Cuisine: Regional, Belgian, French
Located in a 15th-century home in the heart of Bruges, Cafedraal is a trendy restaurant with a beautiful candlelit décor. The restaurant serves some creative variations on regional cuisine such as fried goose liver with apples or an amazing bouillabaisse. An outdoor terrace is available for seating during the summer months.

Cambrinus

....

Philipstockstraat 19
Phone: 32 50 33 23 28
www.cambrinus.eu
Open 11am-11pm
Cuisine: Bar foods, pasta, salads

This restaurant is named for the legendary king of beers, Cambrinus, who was credited with inventing beer itself. Beers are the focal point of the restaurant, which has a significant menu offering everything from snacks and sandwiches to multicourse meals. They even offer something called the "Menu of the Brewers", which includes Trappists' cheese croquettes, Flemish carbonades in "Gulden Draak" beer sauce and a crème brûlée with Dark Abbey beer. It's obvious from the building's façade that it has always had a soft spot for beer. The building was built in 1699 and on one corner of the exterior you will find a statue sitting on a large vat, holding a foaming mug of beer in his hand. Also depicted are Venus, Roman goddess of love, representing spring; Ceres, goddess of agriculture, representing summer; Bacchus, god of wine, representing autumn; and Diana, goddess of the hunt and the moon, representing winter. You will also find the Devil, the Sun and the Moon on the façade.

Celtic Ireland

....

Burg 8
Phone: 32 50 34 45 02
www.celticireland.be
Cuisine: Irish

They say every city had an Irish pub, but Celtic Ireland takes it a step beyond. This family-run establishment pays homage to their homeland and the place is even decorated with scenes from the Book of Kells. In addition to traditional Irish foods, Celtic Ireland has live Irish music nightly.

Charlie Rockets

....

Hoogstraat 19
Phone: 32 50 33 06 60
www.charlierockets.com
Open: Daily 8am-4am
Cuisine: American

Charlie Rockets bills itself as the only American Café in Bruges. Once the home of Bruges' largest theatre it is now a popular café, bar and youth hostel. The place only closes for a few hours each morning to clean up and get ready for the next working day.

Curiosa

Vlamingstraat 22
Phone: 32 50 34 23 34
www.curiosa-brugge.com/English/index_Eng.php
Open: Weekdays, 11.30am-3pm, 4-10.30pm; Saturday, 12-11pm;
Sunday 12-10pm
Cuisine: Regional, Belgian
Initially it was run as a tavern, but in the last 5 years, this medieval cellar has been transformed into a cosy restaurant. Taverne Curiosa has a good selection of beers and wines and offers simple snacks as well as local cuisine featuring meat or fish. On Saturday and Sunday, the Taverne also features an afternoon tea with cakes.

Delicatessen de Westhoek

Noordsandstraat 39
Phone: 32 50 33 60 32
Cuisine: Delicatessen
If you are in the mood for a picnic, this is the shop to come to. Delicatessen de Westhoek has a mouthwatering array of hams, cheeses and sausages as well as homemade dishes, cakes and sweets. Sandwiches are also available.

Delices de Bruges

St-Amandsstraat 27
Phone: 32 50 34 87 69
info@delices-de-bruges.be
www.delices-de-bruges.be
Cuisine: Tearoom
Open: Monday, Tuesday, Thursday-Saturday, 10.30am-6.30pm; Sunday,
2-6pm; closed Wednesday
Known for its sweets, Delices de Bruges is a tearoom to rival all others. It has won awards for its homemade chocolates but is also known for its waffles, crepes, cakes and fondue... and offers a great variety of fun things with which to dip.

Den Dyver on Dijver

Dijver 5
Phone: 32 50 33 60 69
Open: Daily, except Wednesday and Thursday
www.dijver.be
Cuisine: Regional, Belgian

This is a restarant to savour. Family owned and operated, Den Dyver is the perfect place to enjoy a unique take on food pairings. Here, they will pair your dishes with the appropriate beer to accentuate the taste. The chef offers some unique blends of tastes.

Items like duck breast with red pepper sauce or grilled mackerel and pesto sorbet will leave you wishing you could eat more. Reservations are almost a must, even in slower seasons. Den Dyver won the Gold Medal in the Beer and Gastronomy Awards 2007 and it is easy to understand why.

Den Gouden Karpel

Vismarkt 9-10-11 – Phone: 32 50 33 33 89and Huidenvettersplein 4 –
Phone: 32 50 33 34 94
www.Dengoudenkarpel.be
info@Dengoudenkarpel.be
Open: Daily, except Monday
Cuisine: Seafood

It's easy to understand the Golden Karp's popularity. As the name suggests, seafood is the speciality and it's always fresh. The location on Huidenvettersplein is a full sit-down restaurant while the Vismarkt is more of a seafood shop with a small café. It is cash only in the shop. Both offer a wide variety of types of seafood and are prepared in numerous ways. The paella is fabulous and so are the mussels.

Duc de Bourgogne

Huidevettersplein 12
Phone 32 50 33 20 38
info@ducdebourgogne.be
www.ducdebourgogne.be
Open: Daily, 11am-10pm; closed Wednesday
Cuisine: Regional, Belgian, French

Located in a hotel in one of the most recognized locations of Bruges, the restaurant in Duc de Bourgogne is a well-kept secret. You can enjoy world class cuisine while dining overlooking the Dijver Canal.

Erasmus

Wollestraat 35
Phone: 32 50 33 57 81
www.hotelerasmus.com
Cuisine: Regional, Belgian
An exceptional brasserie located within the Erasmus Hotel overlooking Dijver Canal. The restaurant features a creative menu that includes everything from fresh fish and goose to wood pigeon and sweetbreads. They are known for the wide variety of beers brewed and served in small barrels. Tastings are almost essential. The proprietors pride themselves with only serving what they consider to be the results of the artisanship of small Flemish family breweries. The 8-10 draught beers change monthly.

't Brugs Fonduehuisje

WIjngaardstraat 20
Phone: 32 50 33 55 57
www.Fonduehuisje.be
Cuisine: Fondue
As the name suggests, this restaurant is all about fondue. A small establishment, it makes the most of its size and delivers some of the best cheese and chocolate fondue you will ever taste.

De Floren Tijnen

Academiestraat 1
Phone: 32 50 67 75 33
info@deflorentijnen.be
www.deflorentijnen.be
Open: Daily, except Sunday and Monday
Cuisine: Regional, Belgian, French
The restaurant "De Florentijnen" is located in a historic building that was key to trade during Bruges' days as a seaport in the Middle Ages. It has a wonderful menu offering a creative selection of Flemish dishes including meats and sea food. Order a la carte or fixed menu.

El Greco

....

Sint Jacobstraat 48
Phone: 32 50 33 02 96
www.el-greco.be
Open: 5.30pm-1am, live music
Cuisine: Mediterranean, Greek

Authentically Greek, right in the heart of Bruges, El Greco is as much about the atmosphere as it is the food. Live music and even Greek dancing will transport you to another country. And the traditional Greek menu will only add to the feeling that you have momentarily left Bruges. El Greco has been a popular dining and entertainment spot since 1984.

Grand Café Den Comptoir

....

Dijver 13
Phone: 32 50 34 41 54
www.grandcafedencomptoir.be
Cuisine: Belgian, French

This charming brasserie is located right across from the Dijver Canal. It offers small plates as well as fixed menus. Reasonably priced and delightfully elegant décor will only make the meal more enjoyable.

Gruuthuse Hof

....

Mariastraat 35
Phone: 32 50 33 06 14
www.gruuthusehof.be
Open: Daily, except Wednesday and Thursday
Cuisine: Regional

The building is immediately recognizable but don't overlook actually eating here. Gruuthuse Hof has been serving delicious and reasonably priced set meals since 1955.

De Lotus

....

Wapenmakerstraat 5
Phone: 32 50 33 10 78
www.lotus-brugge.be

Open: Daily 11.45am-2pm, closed Sunday
Cuisine: Vegetarian
Bruges' best-known and best-loved vegetarian restaurant, De Lotus has been serving its unique cuisine for more than a quarter of a century. The delicious fare varies according to what is in season.

Marieke Van Brugghe

Mariastraat 17
Phone: 32 50 34 33 66
www.mvb.be
Cuisine: Belgian, French
Located right across from the Church of Our Lady, Marieke Van Brugghe is a popular spot for tourists and locals. Serving both meat and seafood, there is a choice of set menus or a la carte. Specialties include bouillabaisse and Flemish stew with beer. Outdoor seating is also available in warm months.

Mozarthuys Brasserie

Huidevettersplein 1-2
Phone: 32 50 33 45 30
Open: Daily, 6-10.30pm;
closed Wednesday
Cuisine: Stone grilling
Located in a quaint pedestrian square, Mozarthuys is popular year round with locals and visitors. What may set this place apart is the fact that you can choose to cook your own food on a hot lava stone brought to your table. Specialties include meat, fish and scampi on the grill, or mussels and waffles.

Nieuw Museum

Hooistraat 42
Phone: 32 50 33 12 80
www.nieuwmuseum.com
Cuisine: Flemish grill
A combination of trendy dishes in an old world setting, the restaurant's motto is "eat, drink, enjoy!". Nieuw Museum may mean "New Museum" but it has been here more than three decades, specializing in grilled meats and fish, including eel. The aroma of the food alone will entice you.

Oud Handbogenhof

....

Baliestraat 6
Phone: 32 50 33 19 45
Open: From 12pm;
closed Sunday, Monday
Cuisine: Belgian

Oud Handbogenhof is owned by the same people who operate Hotel de Pauw just down the street. Specializing in meat and fish, they pride themselves on using the freshest ingredients possible. In summer you can enjoy your dinner in their beautiful and quiet garden. A special half-board menu is available, but you can also dine a la carte.

Patrick Devos

....

Zilverstraat 41
Phone: 32 50 33 55 66
www.patrickdevos.be
Open: 12-1.30pm, 5pm-9pm;
closed Saturday afternoon, Sunday
Cuisine: Haute Cuisine

Patrick Devos is a gastronomic restaurant in a superb historical building in the centre of the town of Bruges. The elegant Art-Nouveau interior puts you in the mood to really enjoy the rich, inventive and colourful culinary preparations. Chef Patrick Devos lends his name to his restaurant where he changes the cuisine according to the seasons.

Pieter Pourbus

....

Pieter Pourbusstraat 1
Phone: 32 50 34 11 45
www.pieterpourbus.com
Open: Daily, 6-10pm; Saturday, Sunday: also 12-2 pm;
closed Wednesday
Cuisine: Regional, Belgian, French

Another of Bruges' best restaurants, Pieter Pourbus is named after the painter who lived in this historic home during his most prolific years. Built in 1561, it is cosy, largely candlelit and has two open fires. The food and beer are fabulous and reasonably priced. Meat and fish are served with equal flair.

De Republiek

....

Sint-Jakobsstraat 36
Phone: 32 50 34 02 29
www.derepubliek.be
Open: Daily, 11am until the last person leaves
Cuisine: International

Part restaurant, part bar, part cinema, De Republiek has one of the nicest terraces in all of Bruges. Located away from the main tourist area, the food is reasonably priced and plentiful. Hearty soups, moussaka, gazpacho, fajitas and vegetarian meals, this is a popular place to hang out for the late night crowd.

Restaurant Sint-Barbe

....

St Annaplein 29
Phone: 32 50 33 09 99
www.sintbarbe.be
Open: 8:30am-5pm
Cuisine: Tea shop

This small tea shop is located just across the street from St Anne's Church. Saint-Barbe is a pleasant eatery that offers breakfast, lunch or tea. They pride themselves in offering unique dishes but are also known for their incredible homemade chocolates.

Sacré Coeur

....

Langestraat 137
Phone: 32 50 34 10 93
info@sacre.be
www.sacre.be
Open: 12-2pm, 6pm-12am
Cuisine: International

Located in the Sacred Heart Hostel, this restaurant caters to backpackers and those wanting to see the more "relaxed" side of Bruges. Enter into the beating heart of the world of Sacré Coeur. With décor full of reminders of the Flemish collective past, but with a present state of mind and in a contemporary atmosphere, an evening out fast becomes a heartwarming experience. Meals are affordable and include local meat and fish specialties or globally inspired pasta, salads and desserts.

De 7evende Hemel

Walpein 6
Phone: 32 50 33 17 39
Open: Tuesday-Sunday, 11am-9.30pm
Cuisine: Seafood, Belgian, French
The name means Seventh Heaven and you'll understand why when you walk into this rustic, cosy restaurant. The look defies the feel, though because it is managed by a young and ambitious team which gives the place a great energy. The menu varies according to seasons. The restaurant also has a terrace to enjoy in the warmer months.

Tom's Diner

West-Gistelhof 23
Phone: 32 50 33 33 82
www.tomsdiner.be
Open: Daily, from 1pm
Cuisine: Fusion, French, Mediterranean
Located in the quiet St Giles neighbourhood in a historic home, Tom's Diner gets its name from Chef Tom Mestdagh. Small and always busy with locals, it's good to book ahead of time. The food changes per season and offers a wonderful mixture of French and Mediterranean styles.

De Twijfelaar

Eekhoutstraat 24
Phone: 32 50 34 15 44
Open: 12-2.30pm, 6.30pm-12am; closed Sunday, Monday
Cuisine: Belgian, French, Grill
This bistro prides itself on having an artistic touch. The French-Belgian kitchen offers a choice that includes a variety of grilled dishes, filet mignon and gastronomic specialties. Ribs are a speciality, with four different preparations.

La Tavern Brugeoise

Markt 27
Phone: 32 50 33 21 32
www.tavern-brugeoise.be

Open: Monday-Thursday, 9am-6pm; Friday, 9am-5.30pm; Sat, 9am-5pm
Cuisine: Regional
Located directly across from the Belfry on the Grande Place, the Tavern offers regional cuisine. The food is as good as the view. Often crowded because of the location, the fish soup and the mussels are worth the wait. If you prefer something other than seafood, they have a wide choice of menu items.

Verdi

Vlamingstraat 5
Phone: 32 50 34 42 43
www.verdibrugge.com
Open: Daily, except Tuesday
Cuisine: Classic French-Belgian, nouvelle
Located in the Verde Hotel in the St Giles district, the restaurant's décor mixes Spanish and English while the food is mostly classic French-Belgian. The tearoom offers fresh waffles and pancakes.

De Verloren Hoek

Carmerstraat 178
Phone: 32 50 33 06 98
Open: Daily, except Tuesday, Wednesday
Cuisine: Regional
Located near the windmills in a quiet neighbourhood, De Verloren Hoek offers good, home styled meals. The name means "Lost Corner" but you'll soon find that the locals have certainly found this place. The meals are wonderful and very reasonably priced. Don't be surprised if there is some neighbourhood activity taking place.

Restaurant Visscherie

Vismarket 8
Phone: 32 50 33 02 12
info@visschereie.be
www.visscherie.be
Open: Daily, 12-4pm, 5-10pm; closed Tuesday
Cuisine: Seafood
Located across from the fish market, Visscherie has entrances both at the mar-

ket and on Huidevettersplein. Specializing in seafood, they claim to be the first "fish only" restaurant in Bruges. Always fresh, always tasty, their specialties are mussels and eel.

't Volkshuis

Braambergstraat 11
Phone: 32 50 33 80 21
Open: Daily, except Tuesday
Cuisine: Regional, pub
This traditional café and pub is about as local as they come. The food is authentic and so are the sing-alongs, which take place almost every evening. Good value and great lunches.

't Walnutje

Walpein 3/4/5
Phone: 32 50 34 12 45
Cuisine: Regional
Quaint and friendly with an open fireplace 't Walnutje is centrally located. The atmosphere is as good as the food, which is a simple affair.

De Windmolen Bistro

Carmerstraat 135
Phone: 32 50 33 97 39
Cuisine: Regional
De Windmolen Bistro is a very local bar and restaurant and a perfect place to blend in with the people of this quiet neighbourhood who frequent the bistro. You can view the windmills out of the front windows as you enjoy the delicious food. Simple and inexpensive, it's worth the journey to find this place.

De Wijngaert

Wijngaardstraat 15
Phone: 32 50 33 69 18
www.wijngaert.com
Open: Daily, from 11am during the summer; closed Wednesday, Thursday in winter

Cuisine: Flemish grill
Located very close to the Beguinage, this traditional grill house is very welcoming. The grill is just as you come in the door. They serve meat and fish, but if you just want a small snack or coffee, they are willing to accommodate.

De Zolder Keldercafe

53 Vlamingstraat
Phone: 32 4 77 24 49 05
www.keldercafedezolder.be
Hours: Daily from 4pm; closed on Tuesday
Cuisine: pub fare
Located a bit further away from the crowded tourist spots but De Zolder Keldercafe is worth the journey for the atmosphere. This cellar bar/restaurant is known for its beers more than its food. Its menu is limited but impressive. Cosy up next to the fire and enjoy.

Where to Stay

Because Bruges has been so careful to preserve its history, there are dozens of unique hotels located in a historic area. Many are in converted medieval buildings, so don't let what sounds like the name of a hotel chain fool you. Also, because the town appeals to artists and backpackers, there are some very affordable alternatives.

Hotels

De Barge

Bargeweg 15
Phone: 32 50 38 51 50
www.hoteldebarge.be
There is no arguing that this may be Bruges' most unusual hotel. De Barge, once plied the Bruges-Ghent canal as an actual working barge. Today, it is a three-star hotel offering canal views from each of the 22 cabins. Whether you opt for the Captain's Cabin, the Officer's Cabin or a standard luxury cabin, you can expect every comfort, including radio, telephone and TV. De Barge's Restaurant, the Captain's Table is known for its excellent regional cuisine.

Best Western Hotel Acacia

Korte Zilverstraat 3a
Phone: 32 50 34 44 11
www.bestwestern.com
This Bruges hotel has been welcoming guests since 1479. Situated behind the Grand Place, it is close to all major activities in the city. The Best Western Hotel Acacia offers deluxe services and accommodation in singles, doubles, twins, family rooms or suites, including a complimentary full breakfast buffet and courtesy newspaper service. Other hotel amenities include a lounge, a cosy bar, a garden with terrace, free high speed internet, on-site car park, an indoor, heated swimming pool and sauna.

Hotel Academie

Wijngaardstraat 7

Phone: 32 50 33 22 66
www.hotelacademie.be
The Hotel Academie is a modern hotel situated right in the historic "golden tri-angle" of Bruges, just 50 metres from the famous Minnewater (Lake of Love) and the Begijnhof (Beguine Convent). With 82 stylish rooms, the hotel offers all the necessary comforts: air-conditioning, telephone with direct outside line, wake-up service and TV with remote control. Relax in the bar, in the lovely winter garden or on the stylish garden terrace. Discover delicious cuisine and delightful shopping right here in the neighbourhood, while leaving your car in the convenient under-ground parking facility.

Hotel Asiris
....

Lange Raamstraat 9
Phone: 32 50 34 17 24
www.hotelasiris.be
The Asiris Hotel is a restored patrician residence in the shadow of the 15th century St-Gillis church. The 13 rooms include a private bathroom with bath or shower and toilet, radio, TV and telephone. Wake up each morning with a delicious breakfast buffet in the cosy common room. Take a break from sightseeing in the afternoon and unwind with a cup of tea on the garden terrace.

Bonifacius Guesthouse
....

Groeninge 4
Phone: 32 50 49 00 49
www.bonifacius.be
This exclusive private guest house is located on one of Bruges' most picturesque canals. Its sunny waterfront terrace has views of Our Lady Cathedral and Boni-facius gets its name from the Bonifacius bridge that adjoins it. One part of the guesthouse is at water level and is from the Middle Ages, featuring a wooden gable and leaded windows. The other part is from the 16th-century and is situated in a quiet street with cobble stones. Bonifacius' guestrooms radiate an elegant and refined ambiance. All differ in style and character, with authentic and original antiques, objets d'art and elegant fabrics. You stay cocooned in the luxury of a private house and yet enjoy the equipment of a hotel deluxe with extremely high comfort: air conditioning, mini-bar, granite bathrooms with whirlpool, remote con-trol TV, DVD, laptop safe, and free internet access. Breakfast can be taken in the intimacy of the Gothic Room with views onto the canal.

Crown Plaza

....

Burg 10
Phone: 32 50 44 68 44
www.CrownePlaza.com
The Crowne Plaza Hotel Bruges is situated in the city centre, conveniently located on the magnificent Burg Square, adjacent to the historic Town Hall and the Chapel of Holy Blood. Built on the site of St Donaas's Cathedral, which was destroyed by Napoleon in 1799, the remains of the Romanesque choir gallery of the 1,000-year-old church have been incorporated into the lower levels of the hotel. The hotel has 96 fully renovated, air-conditioned rooms with TV, pay TV, iron, coffee and tea facilities, mini bar and safe.

Duc de Bourgogne

....

Huidevettersplein 12
Phone 32 50 33 20 38
www.ducdebourgogne.be
This boutique hotel on the Dijver Canal is situated in one of the most recognized locations of Bruges. The hotel's history goes back to April 27, 1648, when a person named Popieul was given permission to build a new establishment on the Tanner's Square, next to the Tanner's Corporation Guild Hall. Duc de Bourgogne offers just 10 elegant and refined guestrooms. The Duke's restaurant is considered to offer one of the finer dining experiences in Bruges.

English Convent (Engels Klooster)

....

Carmersstraat 85
Phone: 32 50 33 24 24
www.the-english-convent.be
The Engels Klooster offers a unique experience for staying in Bruges. The convent has been here since 1629 and at one time housed a school. Since the school's closing, the nuns have begun making rooms available for overnight guests for meditation, meetings, conferences, courses, study or silent days.

Erasmus

....

Wollestraat 35
Phone: 32 50 33 57 81

www.hotelerasmus.com

A quaint boutique hotel, Erasmus has ten luxury rooms that all enjoy enchanting views overlooking the Dijver Canal. Centrally located and reasonably priced, this is the sort of hotel where you never want to leave. The hotel also prides itself on being environmentally conscious and was one of the first "green" hotels In Flanders. Its restaurant is very popular for both its cuisine and its wide selection of beers.

Flanders Hotel
....

Langestraat 38
Phone: 32 50 33 88 89
www.hotelflanders.com
Flanders Hotel in the heart of Bruges offers four-star accommodation and the ideal base to explore the city. The 41 elegant and well-appointed rooms present guests with a home away from home. The hotel's facilities allow for plenty of relaxation with an indoor heated swimming pool, verdant gardens, Flemish salon and bar and a daily, scrumptious hot and cold breakfast

Hans Memling
....

Kuipersstraat 18
Phone: 32 50 47 12 12
www.hansmemlinghotel.com
The Hans Memling is a three-star hotel, located in the very centre of the city. There are 36 guest rooms, a bar, a garden-terrace and facilities for holding business meetings and seminars. Close to the Markt as well as most shopping.

Koffieboontje
....

Halestraat 4
Phone: 32 50 33 80 27
www.hotel-koffieboonjte.be
Located directly behind the Belfry, Koffieboontje is on a quiet, traffic-free shopping street. The hotel has a contemporary architectural environment with an inner court and sun terrace. All rooms have a private bathroom, telephone, colour TV, hairdryer and free coffee- and tea-making facilities. Bicycle rentals are available on site.

Hotel Jacobs
....

Baliestraat 1
Phone: 32 50 33 98 31
www.hoteljacobs.be
Hotel Jacobs is situated in the quiet and picturesque St Giles neighbourhood. Behind the traditional gabled façade, you will discover a hotel with all the modern comforts. There are 23 rooms in total. The prices depend on the size and comfort of the each. All rooms have en suite bathrooms with bath or shower, TV and telephone. All first, second and third floor rooms are easily accessible with the lift. The spacious breakfast room, a peaceful lounge and a cosy bar are at your disposal.

Hotel Leopold

Hoogste van Brugge 2
Phone: 32 50 33 51 29
www.hotelleopold.be
Hotel Leopold is a comfortable, family-owned two-star hotel, situated at 't Hoogste van Brugge, one of the smallest streets in the medieval town. In addition to the hotel, owners Reginald and Corry offer three elegantly decorated flats in a house close to the hotel. These flats make ideal accommodation for visitors in search of more independence and intimacy than they would find in a more traditional hotel. Flat-suites have a bedroom with two single beds, and a very comfortable collapsible bed for two persons in the living room. There is also an en suite bathroom with shower, toilet, make-up mirror and hairdryer, and a flat-screen TV, free internet connection and safe. A dining corner, fully equipped kitchenette with electric hob, cooking gear, coffee machine, microwave and refrigerator are at your disposal.

Maison le Dragon

Eekhoutstraat 5
Phone: 32 50 72 06 54
www.maisonledragon.be
Located in a 16th-century manor house in the centre of the city, Maison le Dragon includes elegant rooms that are both spacious and clean. This exclusive private guesthouse has been recently renovated and restored to its old glory. You immediately feel at home in the good company of wood-panelling, antiques, engravings, consoles and mirrors. Rooms are accessible by lift or staircase and offer the highest standards of comfort: air conditioning, flat screen TV offering most European Channels, CD- and DVD-player, WIFI, mini bar, safe, direct dial telephone, iron, granite bathrooms with Jacuzzi, hairdryer, make-up mirror, bathrobes, and more.

In the morning, a full breakfast is served in the Louis XVI-cabinet. The sitting room with mural and ceiling paintings from the 18th century in Rococo style invites you to dream away into the past.

Best Western Premier Hotel Navarra

41 St.-Jakobsstraat,
Phone: 32 50 34 05 61
www.bestwestern.com

Navarra is a charming family-run four-star hotel enjoying a prime location in the heart of the historical city centre. This elegant 17th-century listed mansion has recently been completely renovated with great flair and intensive attention to detail. All rooms are spotlessly clean and enjoy air conditioning, a TV, an in-room safe, a trouser press and coffee- and tea-making facilities. A delicious buffet breakfast is complimentary as well as the use of wireless internet access, the indoor pool, sauna and state-of-the-art fitness room. Guests are welcome to relax in the jazz bar "The Duke" or in the peaceful garden. A private car park is at the disposal of guests.

Hotel De Pauw

Sint Gilliskerkhof 8
Phone: 32 50 33 71 18
www.hoteldepauw.be

This delightful small family hotel has just eight rooms and is situated in a quiet quarter overlooking the St Gilles church. Its brick façade is covered in vines and flowerboxes and six of its eight rooms face the church. The rooms are small and inexpensive. The hotel doesn't have a lift. Six of the eight bathrooms were redone in 2007, and now have dark wood panelling, and some have bathtubs. The De Pauw's owners also run the restaurant "Oud Handbogenhof" around the corner, specializing in fish, spare ribs and steaks.

The Pand 4 star

Pandreitje 16
Phone: 32 50 34 05 56
www.pondhotel.be

A member of Small Luxury Hotels in the world as well as Romantik Hotels & Restaurants International, the Pand is located in the carriage house of a 19th-century private mansion. Just a few steps away from the canals, the hotel has 26 bedrooms that have been individually decorated and offer the modern comfort that the discerning traveller expects.

The Family Vanhaecke, which owns the Pand, shares their love of antiques with guests through their elegantly appointed hotel. Guests can relax by the open fire in the library. The Junior Suites include a Jacuzzi, flat screen TV and high quality bodycare products. Full cooked breakfast with waiter service and champagne is served upon white linen table cloths, napkins with embroidered initials and silver teapots. Enjoy the patio, a haven of peace and quiet in the heart of the old city, or the sauna for complete relaxation.

Hotel Portinari

't Zand 15
Phone: 32 50 34 10 34
www.portinari.be
Conveniently located on 't Zand near the railway station and shops, Hotel Portinari is a great base for anyone exploring Bruges. A hotel since the beginning of the 20th century, the four-star Portinari takes its name from Tomasso di Folco Portinari, a wealthy Florentine businessmen who represented the Medici family in Bruges. Rooms are spacious and comfortable and the multinational staff is friendly and welcoming.

Relais Oud Huis Amsterdam

Spiegelrei 3
Phone: 32 50 34 18 10
www.oha.be
The Relais Oud Huis Amsterdam includes 44 rooms located across 5 authentic canal houses from the 17th century. This four-star hotel provides tasteful guest rooms, a peaceful rose garden and many different lounges, offering the charm of its original, historic elements in combination with modern furnishings. Choose to start your day with a delightful champagne breakfast buffet in one of the hotel's lounges.

All rooms and suites have individually been decorated with both antiques and fashionable materials. Enjoy the brand-new, designer bathrooms with luxurious amenities. Situated along one of the nicest canals in Bruges, standard rooms overlook the courtyard and garden while the "privilege" rooms overlook the canal. Wi-Fi is available and there is a computer in the lounge.

Hotel Ter Brughe

....

Oost-Gistelhof 2
Phone: 32 50 34 03 24
www.hotelterbrughe.com

Hotel Ter Brughe is a 16th-century former patrician's house in the late Brugean Gothic style. Located along one of the most picturesque canals in the peaceful old quarter of St Giles near the 14th-century Augustine Bridge, it is only a few minutes away from the city centre. All 46 bedrooms are comfortably furnished and equipped with modern facilities. Breakfast is served in the medieval vaulted cellar. The hotel also offers Wi-Fi (small charge applies).

Hotel De Tuilerieen

....

Dijver 7
Phone: 32 50 34 36 91
www.hoteltuilerieen.com

One of Bruges' premier hotels, Hotel de Tuilerieën is house in a 15th-century mansion in the centre of Bruges. Beautifully lavish period décor and antiques come together with sleek contemporary facilities, superb canal views and indulgent breakfasts. The splendid interior includes a pillared breakfast room with its imposing fireplace, vaulted ceiling and vast crystal chandelier. Most rooms and suites overlook Bruges' most beautiful canal and the city's Renaissance architecture. The champagne breakfast, complete with chocolate fountain, prepares you for the short walk to the city centre. Back at the hotel, a swim in the indoor pool or a sauna refreshes you before dining in the unique restaurant, Le Menu Belge.

Verdi

....

Vlamingstraat 5
Phone: 32 50 34 42 43
www.verdibrugge.com

Located in the St Giles district, Verdi offers suites that include drawing rooms in addition to the bedroom area. The hotel has a wonderful restaurant and private parking available for an extra charge.

Hotel Walwyck

....

Leeuwstraat 8

Phone: 32 50 61 63 60
www.walwyck.com
One of Bruges' newest hotels, it is still located in one of oldest areas, not far from St Jakobs Church next to the lion bridge. The hotel calls itself the "cool down" hotel, saying it is the perfect place to come and just relax. Its modern décor complements the 17th-century building where it is located. There are just 18 rooms, each equipped with a large wardrobe, a flat screen TV and a bathroom with bath or shower. The breakfast room offers an extensive breakfast buffet and Wi-Fi is available in the lounge.

Bed and Breakfast

Alegria Hotel

St Jakobsstraat 34 B-C
Phone: 32 50 33 09 37
www.alegria-hotel.com
Onsite spa treatments only add to the relaxing atmosphere of the Alegria. Owners the De Muynck Family have lived in Bruges for generations and operate this Manor house with inner garden, a coach house and a house with private garage. This quaint boutique bed and breakfast in a quiet neighbourhood very near the Markt affords you the ability to be pampered in a beautiful setting.

Bariseele

Collaert Mansionstraat 1
Phone: 32 4 77 76 00 06
www.bariseele.be
Bariseele is located in a quiet and historic quarter near the 14th-Century St-Gillis Church. In 1930, the guesthouse was a hotel, called hotel Bariseele. It is now a private home with renovated apartments for holiday guestrooms. Rooms are airy, non-smoking, with private shower or bathroom, toilet, hairdryer, private kitchen, toaster, microwave, kettle, minibar, TV and free WiFi-internet. A cot for children up to four years is available on request.

Belfry Bed and Breakfast

Middelburgstraat 6
Phone: 32 50 67 66 79

www.belfry-bedandbreakfast.be

Belfry Bed and Breakfast is located in a quiet little street in the historic centre of Bruges, only a few footsteps away from Markt square, Belfry tower and Burg, in the immediate vicinity of all the cultural events and touristic places you are longing to see. Just around the corner are the main shopping streets and a wide choice of restaurants. Rooms include breakfast as well as tea, coffee and hot chocolate facilities in the kitchen. The guest room is on the ground floor and features TV and internet access, private bathroom with shower, washstand and toilet. Payment is in cash only.

Het Consulaat

Elf Julistraat 27
Phone: 32 4 75 61 77 24
www.hetconsulaat.be
This unique estate used to serve as the honorary consulate of Portugal. Het Consulaat ("The Consulate") offers three renovated rooms with high quality furniture, TV, wireless internet and bathrooms. Guests have a private kitchen and a garage.

Huise 't Schaep

Korte Vuldersstraat 14
Phone: 32 50 34 06 30
www.huishetschaep.be
Huis 't Schaep is a small luxury private guesthouse combined with a small boutique hotel. It is located in one 16th-century and one 17th-century building, which were joined together around 1850. The apartment and the suites at Huis 't Schaep offer tasteful and individual interiors with original elements. They all have comfortable facilities, such as a spacious bathroom with private bath. Close to the cathedral and with all the major tourist attractions, shops and restaurants on your doorstep.

Huyze Ten Hove

10 St Salvator Kerkhof
Phone: 32 50 33 39 59
www.huyzetenhove.be
Owners Marleen and André Uyttenhove-Devriendt offer two beautiful guest rooms in the heart of the city in this charming bed and breakfast. The rooms are luxu-

riously furnished and each has a small lounge area with a TV, fridge and safe hidden in a cupboard. Each morning, the charmingly-laid breakfast table groans with a generous yet refined selection of food and drink, served from chintzy china. Payment is in cash only.

Greets B & B

Julius Delaplacestraat 118
Phone: 32 475 48 00 44
www.bedbreakfastbruges.be
Greets Bed and Breakfast is a privately owned bed and breakfast located at walking distance to the Grande Place. Consisting of one flat located in a manor house, Greets was renovated in 2006. It has a large private living room with ample sitting corner and breakfast corner (refrigerator, water cooker, etc.). TV and internet connection are provided. In addition to a sleeping room with double bed, private shower and toilet, there are two extra beds in a separate room. Moderate prices. Free and safe car parking in the street; bicycles at your disposal.

Hostels

Charlie Rockets

Hoogstraat 19
Phone: 32 50 33 06 60
www.charlierockets.com
Charlie Rockets is home to not just a hostel but to one of the most popular bars around for backpackers. Once the home of Bruges' largest cinema it is now has both dormitories and double rooms available. Affordable and centrally located, linens are included and internet is available. Downstairs, the bar and restaurant remain open 8-4am each day.

Lybeer's Traveller's Hostel

Korte Vuldersstraat 31
Phone: 32 50 33 43 55
www.hostellybeer.com
Formerly a Catholic rectory, Lybeers offers a quiet and affordable retreat for those exploring Bruges. The property includes both dormitory rooms and private guest rooms. Bed linen is provided. Rooms vary from single to quadruple with en suite

or shared facilities. Deep baths with showers on every floor, some ensuite. Free internet.

St Christopher's Bauhaus

Langestraat 133-137
Phone: 32 50 34 10 93
www.bauhaus.be

The St Christopher's Bauhaus is a charming hostel, budget hotel and holiday apartment that has something for everyone, with many free extras. Enjoy your stay in authentic "Bruges style" beautifully restored, step-gabled houses, which were recently turned into comfortable and very affordable accommodation. They boast a wealth of services for all travellers and needs. Rooms at the Bauhaus Hostel range from dormitories of five, six and eight beds, to four persons, triples and private doubles. Showers and toilets provided centrally. Sheets, pillows and duvets are provided at no extra cost. Private rooms with showers are part of the budget hotel. Group rentals (up to 22 people) are available in the holiday apartment.

Events

As if there wasn't enough to experience in Bruges already, the city is also known for its festivals and celebrations. If you are uncertain when you should plan your visit, maybe this list will help you find something that you might want to experience. The Department of Tourism (In&Uit Brugge [Concertgebouw]), located at 't Zand can give you more information.

Weekly Events

't Zand Market
Saturday 7am-1pm
Just about any and everything gets sold. Food, rugs, plants, clothes, you name it. The market is located mostly in the centrally located 't Zand market, but also stretches on to nearby Boeveriestraat.

El Mundo - Multicultural Café
Friday 8pm
Weekly on Friday at Vlamingstraat 55

Flea Market
Saturday & Sunday 10am-6pm (March 15–November 15).
Flea market along Dijver and at Fish Market

Gregorian's Mass
Sunday 10am
Paters Karmelieten (Carmelite Church)
Location: Ezelstraat 28

Lazy Sundays: Live blues, jazz, boogie
Sunday 7.30pm
Location: Wijnbar Est, Braambergstraat 7

Football (Jupiler League)
Weekly
Bruges has two teams in the premier league (Jupiler League): FC Bruges and Cercle Bruges. Both teams play their home games in the Jan Breydelstatdion in Sint-Andries, about 5km (3mi) from the centre of town. Easy transportation is

available by bus departing at the railway station or Zand Square. Check schedules at www.clubbrugge.be.

Annual Events

January
....

January 1
New Year's Day Carillon
Location: Markt

The New Year is rung in annually with a carillon concert in the Markt Square. Wrap up warmly and listen to the beautiful music of the 47 bells of the belfry tower.

Early January
Snow and Ice Sculpture Festival
Location: Stationsplein
www.iccscuplture.be

The Snow and Ice Sculpture Festival opens ice gates on the Station Square in Bruges in late November and continues through to early January. It was Europe's first indoor Snow and Ice Sculpture Festival when it started in 2000. Thanks to state-of-the-art refrigeration and isolation technology, it is possible to keep a specially-built 1,350m² ice tent at a constant temperature of -5° C. More than 400 tons of snow and ice are shipped in and professional sculptors create exquisite pieces according to each year's theme.

February
....

No major events in February

March
....

Mid- March
Cinema Novo Festival
Location: Lumiere Cinema and the Liberty
www.cinemanovo.be/en

Bruges' Cinema Novo Film Festival presents new non-commercial films from Africa, Asia and Latin America. The festival also invites some filmmakers to present their work.

April

Last weekend in April
Meifoor
Location: 't Zand, Albertpark, Beursplein en Simon Stevinplein
Called a "Fun Fair", this is a festival to welcome spring.

May

May 1
Red Rock Rally
Location: Astridpark
www.redrockrall.be
Begun in 1995, the Red Rock Rally is a free rock concert and outdoor party that celebrates workers' day in Astridpark on May 1 every year.

First Weekend in May
The Chocolate Festival - Choco-laté
Location: Museum of Bruges – Belfort, Markt 7
www.choco-late.be
Bruges claims to be the capital of Belgian chocolate and this event is a chocolate lover's dream. There are displays and sampling of all things chocolate as chocolatiers from throughout Bruges show off their talents.

Early May
Inside Bruges
www.excellentconcept.com
Inside Bruges is an interior design event where visitors follow a design trail through the city in a walking tour of the design competition. Interior designers, antique dealers, artists and florists all participate. Visitors explore Bruges' narrow cobbled streets, travelling along the canals into convents, contemporary lofts and even private mansions.

Ascension Day
Procession of the Holy Blood
Location: Burg
www.holyblood.org
This procession of the Holy Blood has taken place in Bruges every year on Ascension Day since 1291. The colourful parade includes depictions of the Old and New

Testament as well as a display of the purported relic of the blood of Jesus, which is normally kept in the Church of the Holy Blood located in the Burg.

June

No major events in June.

July

Early July
Zandfeesten (flea market)
Location: Koning Albertpark & 't Zand
Information: Eric Lowyck,
tel. 32 50 34 17 36
www.hgk-bruggewest.com
Held several times a year, this is the biggest flea market in Flanders and is a must for collectors and bargain hunters.

Mid July
Cactus Festival
Location: Minnewaterpark
www.cactusfestival.be
This three-day music festival has been bringing in an eclectic group of internationally known musicians since the mid 1980s.

Mid July
Brugge Tripel Dagen
Location: Markt
www.comitevoorinitiatief.be
Bruges Triple Days are three days of fun and music on Bruges' Market Square. Open to everyone, this festival includes music, food and local artists.

Late July-Early August
Klinkers
Location: Central Bruges
www.klinkers-brugge.be
A series of contemporary music concerts that take place at venues throughout the city. Dancing is encouraged, with music that includes flamenco, tango and klezmer.

August

....

Early August
Musica Antiqua - Early Music Festival of Flanders (MAFestival)
Location: Central Bruges
www.mafestival.be
The Modern Times in Early Music Festival explores how early music is still relevant in modern days and affects present day music. The festival programme also offers lectures, introductions to the concerts and a course on the theme of that years' festival. Music styles include those of the Caribbean, South and Central America, Europe and Africa.

Early August
Benenwerk
Location: Central Bruges
www.benenwerk.be
Benenwerk means "legwork" and this dance festival transforms the entire city into a ballroom. Stages are set up for instructors to give lessons in a wide variety of styles. You can change styles and eras by simply changing locations.

Mid August
Reiefeest - Canalside Festival
Location: Canals throughout Bruges
www.reiefeest.be
A series of impressive historic performances and pageants along the illuminated canalsides for the annual Reiefeest.

A staggering 600 musicians, singers and dancers turn out in elaborate costumes to perform scenes that recapture the spirit and the atmosphere of the Middle Ages, the Renaissance Era and the Baroque Age.

Strolling from one canal to another, visitors encounter Bakelandt's band of thieves, a 19th-century wedding party and the flight of Charles II to Bruges after Cromwell banished him from Britain.

Mid August
Brugse Kantdagen - Lace Days
Location: De Halve Moon Brewery
www.kantcentrum.be
This two-day exhibition and sales event combines two of Bruges' best-loved creations—lace and beer.

September
....

Early September
Open Monumentendag - Heritage Day
www.erfgoedcelbrugge.be
Part of an event held throughout Flanders, the first full weekend in September is used to commemorate local heritage with historical demonstrations as well as access to historic buildings not normally opened to the public.

Mid September
Kroenkelen
Location: Throughout Bruges
www.brugge.be/kroenkelen
Car-free day in Bruges. This is a mass event that promotes walking and cycling trips with music and entertainment along the route.

Late September
Zandfeesten (flea market)
Location: Koning Albertpark and 't Zand,
www.hgk-bruggewest.com
Held several times a year, this is the biggest flea market in Flanders and is a must for collectors and bargain hunters.

October
....

Mid October
Jazz Brugge
Location: Groeninge Museum and Concertgebouw
www.jazzbrugge.be
Jazz Brugge brings jazz performers from all over Europe to Bruges.

November
....

First week in November
Jonge Snaken Festival
Location: Throughout Bruges
www.dewerf.be
The eight-day Young Snake Festival combines music and performance to help get children involved with jazz music.

Early November
Bruges Festival of World Music
Location: Throughout Bruges
The Bruges Festival of World Music offers hot international music to warm the cold winter days.

Mid November
Beer Festival
Location: Belfry Hall, Markt
www.brugsbierfestival.be
Bruges celebrates its history of being a town of brewers by bringing out the best for visitors to partake. More than 150 types of beers can be sampled at this two-day event, which also includes beer cuisine and beer lectures.

Late November-December 31
Christmas Market
Location: Markt
An open-air ice rink with Christmas tree are at the centre of this colourful Christmas tradition. The Markt Square is transformed into a huge market of handmade items, beautifully packaged chocolates and unusual trinkets.

Late November-Early January
Snow and Ice Sculpture Festival
Location: Stationsplein
www.icescuplture.be
The Snow and Ice Sculpture Festival opens ice gates on the Station Square in Bruges in late November and continues through to early January. It was Europe's first indoor Snow and Ice Sculpture Festival when it started in 2000. Thanks to state-of-the-art refrigeration and isolation technology, it is possible to keep a specially-built 1,350m² ice tent at a constant temperature of -5° C. More than 400 tons of snow and ice are shipped in and professional sculptors create exquisite pieces according to each year's theme.

December

Late November-December 31
Christmas Market
Location: Markt
An open-air ice rink with Christmas tree are at the centre of this colourful Christ-

mas tradition. The Markt Square is transformed into a huge market of handmade items, beautifully packaged chocolates and unusual trinkets.

Late November – Early January
Snow and Ice Sculpture Festival
Location: Stationsplein
www.icescuplture.be
The Snow and Ice Sculpture Festival opens ice gates on the Station Square in Bruges in late November and continues through to early January. It was Europe's first indoor Snow and Ice Sculpture Festival when it started in 2000. Thanks to state-of-the-art refrigeration and isolation technology, it is possible to keep a specially-built 1,350m² ice tent at a constant temperature of -5° C. More than 400 tons of snow and ice are shipped in and professional sculptors create exquisite pieces according to each year's theme.

Mid December
December Dance
Location: Various Venues
www.decemberdance.be
December Dance is the latest addition to Bruges' festival landscape. Created by Belgian choreographer Sidi Larbi Cherkaoui, the performances are a mix of old and new pieces, intimately linked to music, most of which is performed live. Dance legends from throughout the world come to perform.

Breinigsville, PA USA
27 November 2010
250182BV00004B/7/P